TO LOVE YOU

The Story of Sister Lynda and a Community

The letter to the Hebrews, speaking of those who show us faith, says of them, "of whom the world was not worthy". Sister Lynda was one of these. To have known her with her faith, smile, song and acute sense of truth (and the ridiculous and pompous!) was to have known someone in whose presence you could sometimes glimpse heaven.

This book, so lovingly written by her companions in the Sisters of Jesus Way, speaks of her faith and love and hope, which she lived facing terminal cancer at 47 years old. We are given a window into Lynda's honesty and pain as well as joy. One of the songs she chose for her funeral included, "We shall know and we shall love." To read this book is to be given the chance to know Sister Lynda and the one in whom she placed her trust, Jesus Christ. She, like him, was called to death too soon. Her greatest joy would be that through reading her story, we might come to know his life.

The Rt Rev. Keith Sinclair
The Bishop of Birkenhead

The compassionate face of Jesus shines out of the pages of this book – through the life of Lynda and her extraordinary faith; through a remarkable community which takes astonishing risks in faithfulness to the call of God; and through joy, pain, unanswered questions and death. It tells the story of lives touched by the love of God and the power of the Holy Spirit. I have been one of many whose life has been enriched by Lynda and the Sisters of Jesus Way. This book opens their story to many more and shows how powerfully God can work in the lives of women and men today.

The Rev. Professor David Wilkinson
Principal, St John's College,
University of Durham

Sister Lynda was one of the jewels at the heart of the very special place and ministry that is the Jesus Way. I have been one of those fortunate in being able to draw on it as a resource for reflection, prayer and refreshment for almost as long as Lynda was part of it – certainly back to the Lang Lane days. Beyond Lynda's winsome sweetness and ready laughter there was a parable of commitment to a different sort of lifestyle and purpose than she might well have chosen. She was certainly intelligent and capable. But this story, lovingly told by her companions on the journey, describes how she became an epitome of joyful service to her Lord, and not without struggle. For fewer years than we would have wished she was a shining example of how someone can reflect "the glory of God in the face of Jesus Christ" (2 Cor. 4:6).

The Ven. Ricky Panter
The Archdeacon of Liverpool

This is an honest account about the lives of the Sisters of Jesus Way; how God led them, and particularly Sister Lynda, to the Community.

I first met Sister Lynda in 2002 in my capacity as Hospital Chaplain. I appreciated and valued the visits of the Sisters, who became firm Christian colleagues and friends. Lynda visited the wards of the Clatterbridge Centre for Oncology on Sunday mornings with Sister Marie, playing the guitar and singing – with her pure, clear voice – their favourite hymns and songs which brought comfort, hope and joy. The patients said it was like listening to an angel. The words of Lynda's songs live on through the pages of this book.

The Rev. Dave Nugent
Chaplain to Clatterbridge Cancer Centre

TO LOVE YOU ONLY

The Story of Sister Lynda and a Community

CHURCH IN THE MARKET PLACE PUBLICATIONS

2013

Church in the Market Place Publications

Plate section:

All photos on first page and all photos of Lynda on second page
© Glenys and Merfyn Jones

Photo of Rev. Brian Galliers on second page © Mrs Una Galliers

Photos at top left and at bottom of eighth page © Liz Roberts

Photo of our Community at top of tenth page © D. Isenring

Photo of Lynda on final page © Graeme Skinner

All other photos © Sisters of Jesus Way 2013

British Library Cataloguing in Publication Data
A record for this book is available from the British Library

ISBN 978-1-899147-97-7

Typeset in Bookman Old Style
by RefineCatch Ltd, Bungay, Suffolk

Printed in Great Britain by
Cambrian Printers, Aberystwyth

Contents

Dedication

To the late Rev. Brian J. N. Galliers,
and to J. Mason Porter,
in both of whom, through the years, we have seen
the simplicity of the Gospel and the humility of Jesus

FOREWORD

Life, in all its forms, is a journey, whether we speak of the universe as a whole, or our particular life, the unique but finite opportunity which God has granted to us. We all like the periods of stability, where we rely on home and family and friends, the familiarity with which life began in the womb, but these are only resting places on the journey of life.

The story of the Sisters of Jesus Way is just that; the story of a community which is on the move – on the way – with God. The basis of the Community is that the Heavenly Father will provide, as he has unfailingly done over the years. Familiarity with God requires that we accept, and rejoice in, our fragility before Him.

This book is a tribute to the Community, and to the vital part which Sister Lynda played in its development. It is also a powerful witness to the frailty and fragility of the world for which Jesus gave his life unto death.

The consecrated life is a gift to the Church, and thence to the world, as a reminder of God's underlying purposes for his creation. The consecrated life, with its variously framed vows, points to the vision of Paradise in the Garden of Eden, when Adam and Eve owned everything and nothing, where obedience to God was their natural state, and before the possessive complications for human sexuality after the Fall. As such, communities such as the Sisters of Jesus Way are a powerful signpost on our journey to the new heaven and new earth, which God promises to us, in his direct presence.

Sister Lynda has travelled that road, with great grace. May she encourage us as we tread the same path.

The Rt Rev. Dr Peter Forster
The Bishop of Chester

Acknowledgements

We are grateful to Mrs Dorothy Toth on Holy Island and Mother Mary Luke and the Sisters of the Holy Cross in Costock, Nottinghamshire for giving a place of quiet and peace to write.

We are grateful to all those who have encouraged us, especially Sister Lynda's parents, Glenys and Merfyn Jones. Our vicar, Rev. Graeme Skinner and associate vicar, Rev. Martin Daly gave us unfailing support and advice. Cynthia Hinton spent hours assisting us, typing and correcting the manuscript many times, and Dorinda King willingly came to our aid when she was here for a retreat. Sally Shand and Pat Bell patiently proofread for us. There are many others and to all of you, a very big thank-you.

We have appreciated all those who have contributed by making possible quotations from their letters, emails and conversations and those who have loved and prayed us through the time it took to write this book and all that happened immediately before.

Thank you to Michelle and Jim Earlam who in God's perfect timing helped to make the launching of this book possible and Rev. Dan Paterson who acted as our representative in order to find a publisher. We are grateful that he discovered Rev. Robert Davies, a retired Methodist minister, who has safely guided us through to publication.

All quotations at the beginning of each chapter are taken from the "Rule of Life of the Sisters of Jesus Way", unless otherwise stated.

Every attempt has been made to trace all quotations. We apologise for the one quotation that we were unable to trace and for any in the text of Sister Lynda's diaries that we inadvertently missed.

Introduction

We are grateful to the Lord that we shared 26 years of pilgrimage with Sister Lynda of the Compassionate Face of Jesus before he called her home at the early age of 47 on 13th May 2011. In sharing the story of her life, we also share the life of our community, as Lynda lived through our early years until through the mercy of God we became established. We are bound together in Christ and not even death can divide us. We have endeavoured to write it as it really was and is, as Lynda would have wished.

We hope that those who read this book will take courage and inspiration from a life, not without difficulties, but which had many joys and of which Sister Lynda said at the end, "I want you to know that I have no regrets, it has been a good life."

From sunrise to sunset our day is holy,
for Christ has risen from the tomb
and scattered the darkness of death
with light that will not fade.
And though the night will overtake our day
you summon us to live in endless light,
the never ceasing Sabbath of the Lord.[1]

The Sisters of Jesus Way

Early Years and the Journey Begins

"We are children of the Heavenly Father and our security is in him."

In the early hours of the morning on the 30th December 1963 Glenys Jones was driven by her father through dark lanes and roads to the hospital in Wrexham (Wrecsam), a town tucked just inside Wales and close to the English border. Her husband Merfyn was in Bridgend, South Wales, on police training. A few hours after arriving at Maelor Hospital Lynda Jane, their first child, made her entry into the world. By the time Merfyn returned home the following weekend, the jaundice with which she had begun life had cleared. He was delighted to be introduced to his daughter. There was excitement too in the wider circle of the family. Her aunt Maifun wrote to her many years later, "When you were born I was so proud to go to school and tell everyone that I was an auntie; you were special to me." Twenty months later her brother Philip was born. Like all children they squabbled at times but she loved her younger brother and loyally stuck by him. When parental wrath was roused after some mischief she tried to protect him from trouble.

At the same time, the Lord was preparing two young deaconesses for a call that was to come many years later – to found a community, "Sisters of Jesus Way". One of them was working in caravan evangelism on the Welsh/English border. The following April her ordination to the "life and work of a deaconess in the Methodist Church",[1] would take place and she keenly anticipated this after three years as a probationer. The other was a student completing her training at the Wesley Deaconess College in Ilkley. There was no choice in what was called stationing and they were appointed to work together in September 1964. Their first mission was in Shrivenham, a small village in Wiltshire. Their home was a caravan named Pathfinder. To their delight, and it must be confessed their astonishment, they saw the Holy Spirit transforming the lives of several key members of the small Methodist Society. Their preaching was simple and to the point. Jesus died for sinners. Through repentance the Kingdom of God was at hand and a new birth in Christ was possible to those who had faith in him.

They were appointed after three years to different work and were many miles apart but remained friends. Apart from a second stint on caravans for one of them, they lived alone and experienced first-hand the difficulties this can bring for those in full time church work. Very different in temperament, they followed the same path spiritually. Both were influenced by the Renewal of the late sixties and early seventies that broke the dreary, dry theological liberalism of the day. They saw the Holy Spirit working in power and became convinced not only of the new birth in Christ but the necessity of an infilling of the Holy Spirit. They could hardly deny what they saw happening in front of their eyes – prophecy, praying in tongues, healing, to mention a few of the gifts given by God. Their lives were invigorated and changed. Life was now an adventure with the Holy Spirit. While all this was happening the Lord was skilfully weaving the threads that were to bring four Sisters together as the foundation for the Sisters of Jesus Way: a teenager growing up in Edinburgh, the two deaconesses, and Lynda, who was still a young child but who, in this community, was one day to find her home.

Despite geographically being so close to England, and nearby Chester (in England) being helpful for shopping, Lynda grew up as a Welsh child. Her education was in the national language, her family were also Welsh-speaking and the culture was one of music, at which she excelled, and poetry. She competed at Eisteddfodau playing the piano. There was a certain reserve that is often seen in those from North Wales and a melancholy deep in the psyche coming from conquest by the powerful English centuries before. The dark, brooding mountains speak of a hidden past; music is often in the minor key and the poetry, mystically beautiful. Lynda even looked Welsh with her dark hair and grey-blue eyes.

She was sensitive. Some things that those of a more robust nature would have taken in their stride she found painful. Her family moved house a number of times and she approached each new school that she had to attend with increasing dread. She lay awake at night, the fears gathering. When her father resigned from the police the German shepherd dog that her father handled had to be given back. She could never forget his anguished eyes appealing to them from the van as he was driven away. It was this sensitive nature that later in life, yielded to the Lord, enabled her to come alongside others in their need.

Her anxieties dissipated when she was with her nain (grandmother). As a wriggling six-year-old she sat on Nain's lap by the fire while she deftly twisted old strips of rag around her hair to make ringlets. Lynda and her brother spent many happy holidays with their nain and taid (grandfather). As children they loved to dive into and run through the long grass in the meadows by their home.

After primary school she attended a Welsh High School. The use of English was frowned upon even in the staff room. Every subject was taught in Welsh. She was gifted in languages. Her French teacher at Ysgol Morgan Lloyd, the High School, said of her, "one of my two best pupils ever". But all was not well with her at school. She was talented and good-looking. This caused jealousy in some of the other girls. She didn't realise at the time the cause of the difficulties and blamed herself. Her sensitive nature made her more vulnerable than most. An email from a student three years ahead of her, who she had met by chance on a train when she was a Sister, described her as "a very dear person". She did not see herself in that light. There was one person who she knew loved her and that was her grandmother. Lynda describes her nain as being "a steady rock in an uncertain sea", during those difficult years.

3

Every journey has a beginning: for Lynda it was the personal journey of her life in Christ, and for the community, the journey of a life together in Christ. Beginnings are not always where we think they are, as the Holy Spirit prepares the way long before we are aware of his presence. Sometimes it is an acute sense of our own need that opens our eyes. So it was with Lynda. She aimed for the highest in every music examination she took and every eisteddfod that she entered. Mostly she achieved it but the cost in nervous energy was considerable. She had attended a Welsh Chapel Sunday School, and chapels or churches as the family moved, but they had failed to leave any impression on her seeking mind. She often recalled that, when she was about fourteen, she saw a nun in the distance. There was a powerful impression that this would be her calling, even though at the time she was uncertain about God. She never forgot, however, that encounter.

She thought deeply, especially for one so young:

I can say that it was the grace of God which, in my early teens, led me to take a long, hard look at life and come to the same conclusion as the writer of Ecclesiastes – life was utterly empty and meaningless unless there was something more? – in this desolate and very dark period of my life – God, the Creator of the universe and life revealed himself to me through the Lord Jesus – he revealed to me that he is life's meaning. I was filled with hope and purpose as I took my first stumbling steps (into faith).

When her O-Level examinations (and she was entered for ten subjects) loomed on the horizon, the pressures built up. Fear of failure, over-conscientiousness, and difficulties in relationships all came together and she broke down. Again she began to turn towards God. Now in her despair and depression she turned to a woman who she knew to be a Christian. This friend, much older than herself, remembers Lynda then "as rather nervous in disposition", and she spoke to her about Christ as the Rock. She then introduced Lynda to a young Christian girl who was part of a lively youth group at Regent Street Methodist Church in Wrexham. It was an English speaking church. The new friend took Lynda first to a service and then introduced her to the youth group. There was no sudden conversion experience but from that time on Lynda gradually turned towards the light of the Lord.

The Heavenly Father had his hand on his child. The way was gentle into the Kingdom of his beloved Son. The deaconess working at the church was Sister Christine Walters who watched over this "shy and very fragile teenager". Both Sister Christine and her colleague Rev. Alan Cliff had been influenced by the Renewal. There were many keen Christians in the youth group and the Holy Spirit was obviously at work there. Sister Christine realised that Lynda needed to be shielded from the over-enthusiastic amongst them. She writes:

> Lynda was a thoughtful and intelligent person, even in those days. I remember her, as seeming to be at the edge of the crowd for some while and then suddenly she joined in with the other young people, though still with her shyness. I realised that Lynda was very thoughtfully and intelligently deciding who Jesus was and his call to allow him to love her. I tried to stop some of those who were more sure and confident from pushing her along at their speed. There was something very beautiful about her discovery of Jesus because it was at a deeper level than many others. Contemplation was a natural way for her, and, as she had some (what she perceived as) concern/opposition about involvement with the church, Lynda needed to go at her own pace.

Sister Christine and the young people gave her the background of love and support that she needed. Christine spoke also of:

. . . her growth in relationship with people at that time. As she found a deeper trust and friendship in Jesus, so the Holy Spirit seemed to give her more ease with and trust in people.

Now she not only knew the Lord Jesus but she also had friends. Some of the young men in the group were delighted that such a beautiful girl had appeared in their midst. Deep down, however, her heart was already given to the divine Lover.

She moved on educationally to Yale Sixth Form College and she had Christian friends at school. Following her love of languages she studied German and French with English as her third subject. It was the German language that became the greatest love. To many of us she seemed to speak other languages effortlessly but of course this was not the whole picture, there was much hard work. She was, however, blessed with a prodigious memory and a keen ear.

She continued to attend the youth group and worship at Regent Street Methodist, Wrexham. She began to seriously consider that God might have a plan for her life. Again it was Sister Christine who gave the needed support and direction. In a surviving letter dated 17th July 1981 she writes:

I pray that Jesus will become more and more real to you. You are a very special person – greatly loved and treasured in his sight. Always remember that and know that He is with you and will guide you to where He needs you in life. Have courage to follow – those He chooses, He equips for all that lies ahead.

A neighbour who had lived next door to the Jones family met Lynda again when a group of young people were gathered in someone's house. "I left with the feeling that there was something special about her," was his comment.

In her second year at Sixth Form College on 10th January 1982 she became a member of the Methodist Church. This corresponded to the Church in Wales service of confirmation. This was not undertaken lightly. The promise she made that January Sunday "to obey Christ and serve him in the church and in the world",[2] she lived the remainder of her life.

While all this was happening in Lynda's life, the journey was beginning for the Sisters of Jesus Way. The Holy Spirit had been preparing the way for years but now unexpectedly it happened with almost breath-taking speed. One of the two deaconesses had had vague thoughts about a community and a house of the love of God. It would not even merit being described as a vision or as a call. Nine years had passed since they had partnered each other on caravan missions. They spent a week together and talked about the possibility of founding a community. As they prayed and sought God's guidance, suddenly, it seemed right. Now was the time.

They were still under the authority of the Wesley Deaconess Order. So they travelled to Birmingham to seek permission to come out of circuit work and follow wherever the Lord led. Consent was not a foregone conclusion. In fact it seemed to them that it was very unlikely permission would be given. They realised that they would have to "live by faith", as it is commonly known. Not unnaturally most of the mainline denominations, having seen many come unstuck on that road, are not too keen on the idea. They were not so keen on the idea either but there was no other way. The Methodist Church would no longer employ them. Trusting in the providence of the Heavenly Father was the teaching of Jesus: "Seek first his kingdom and his righteousness, and all these things shall be yours as well."[3] Taking the truth in this verse quite literally, alongside the preceding verses where Jesus taught that the Heavenly Father will clothe us and feed us, the meaning is crystal clear.

Also Methodism had no experience of a community such as they were envisioning. To the present day the Sisters are not drawn to the wording "Religious Order" or "a Religious" but, as a Roman Catholic monk pointed out to one of founders, all the hallmarks were there from the beginning. Many years

7

later, when the Sisters of Jesus Way was established, a similar conversation took place with the Bishop of Chester, who said in effect that if the characteristics of a Religious Order were there, whatever we liked to call ourselves, we were one. It isn't surprising that Methodists did not understand. It was outside their experience. The two deaconesses were feeling their way, as it was outside their experience too. It does explain why Lynda's first vague sense of a call was when she glimpsed a nun.

At that time Rev. Brian Galliers was the Warden of the Wesley Deaconess Order. He was a humble and godly man. It was the providence of God that he was the Warden at that time. He gave them cautious permission to follow this call. He was to prove to be a good and wise friend through the years, eventually becoming Chair of our Trust. He asked them to write an "Intention". The foundations were laid not in fact but in their thinking. The Lord Jesus would be our first love. This was our calling, to love him. The Sisters would live and work together. It would be a life of prayer and providing hospitality in such a way that those who stayed would meet with Jesus.

The phrase, "living by faith", was jettisoned. Instead they spoke of trusting the Heavenly Father and making all their needs known to him in prayer. They knew this way had to be followed with integrity. Their paid employment would end. Any insurance was relinquished and their small personal bank accounts were merged into a community fund. They decided that no claim would be made on the state or the church for benefits or grants and no fundraising would be allowed. It was agreed that even hinting about any needs was forbidden! Instead they would pray to their Heavenly Father. There was no back door if it all went wrong, no safety net, as the world sees it.

Brian Galliers kept an anxious eye on all that was happening. Because of his position he had to stay somewhat detached but, as they discovered later, he was desperately hoping the venture would succeed. By this time both deaconesses were in West Yorkshire, as one of them had completed her appointment in Portsmouth and the other had two years still to do in the Cleckheaton and Heckmondwyke circuit. The house where they were living went with the job so their greatest need was somewhere to live when they left there. They felt that the Lord was saying to pray for a large residence so that they could accommodate guests, as well as a community. Time was beginning to run out before they saw their prayers being answered.

In Liverpool a Methodist minister, Rev. Dr Bill Davies, decided to visit a bookshop. While he was there he met an old friend, Mason Porter. In the course of the conversation, Mason said that he was hoping to move with his wife to a smaller house and did he know of any group of people who could use his present house for Christian work? Although the deaconesses had not expressed their need to anyone, Dr Davies knew them and thought that they would possibly be interested. That evening he rang the manse in West Yorkshire and spoke to one of them. The following Sunday she visited the Wirral. The house she saw seemed perfect. Everyone was delighted: the owners, Brian Galliers and the two concerned. No one doubted for one minute that this was the house that the Father had prepared for his community. However, it was not to be, although all that happened at that time was very much part of God's plan. So began the first of many lessons in patience and trust when everything appears to go wrong.

A legal difficulty was encountered which in the end brought everything to a halt. The house was leasehold and written into the lease was a clause that said the building could only be used as a private residence. Many months were spent trying to overcome the problem, but all to no avail. Time was not just running out by now, it actually ran out. Homelessness and failure beckoned.

Does God answer prayer? Some would say that he didn't. Brian Galliers came to their aid and as an interim measure the budding community moved to Manchester for twelve months. A Methodist minister had taken ill and they were to take charge of his four churches for a year. The fact that the

Manse in Droylsden had no furniture, and neither did they, posed a problem but the kind Yorkshire folk saw them through that difficulty. They "sold" them all the furniture in the manse in West Yorkshire for only £5.

It was while they were in Manchester that they reluctantly had to accept that there was no way through the problem over the lease. The Father had closed the door. It was not his will. It was a good lesson to learn although not easy at the time. God has a reason behind disappointments. They were invited to visit West Kirby, a little town on the edge of the Dee estuary overlooked by the Welsh hills. Mason and Nora Porter, who had wanted them to have their house and who lived in that area, showed them several other houses. One of them was a large semi-detached with four floors, large rooms and plenty of potential.

Around the door there was a vine and this seemed an indication that this was the house. Some two years before, they had been given a verse from Deuteronomy:

For the Lord your God is bringing you into a good land, a land of brooks of water, of fountains and springs, flowing forth in valleys and hills, a land of wheat and barley, of vines and fig trees and pomegranates, a land of olive trees and honey, a land in which you will eat bread without scarcity, in which you will lack nothing.[4]

That afternoon the house was purchased and given to them. Despite many years travelling the country, the Wirral had never been on their itinerary. The Heavenly Father had chosen well. The house was minutes from the sea and beautiful views, was near to long walks over gorse-covered hills, pleasant in every season and yet at the same time the location was accessible by both road and rail. The Holy Spirit had begun to teach the simplicity of trusting in God, a simplicity that had been lost in their leadership roles in churches.

A Time of Preparation

"First love for Jesus is a reckless love willing to leave behind security as the world sees it, family, friends and country. 'I tell you the truth,' Jesus replied, 'no one who has left home or brothers or sisters or mother or father or children or fields for me and the gospel will fail to receive a hundred times as much in the present age (homes, brothers, sisters, mothers, children and fields – and with them persecutions) and in the age to come, eternal life.'"[1]

Thus it was that, in September 1979, a large, hired van made a double journey from Manchester and all the worldly possessions of a community newly born, Sisters of Jesus Way, were unloaded and carried into the beautiful, airy house in Lang Lane, West Kirby, Wirral. We had already decided to wear a simple blue dress. The headscarf came later. It was never meant to be a religious habit. We had been called to a life of simplicity and this was one way that we could express that. There was no more shopping in order to find clothes for special occasions and no more dithering as to what to wear in the morning – freedom indeed. It was more than that; it was a little sign that it is the Lord Jesus who makes us happy, not the latest fashions and a crammed wardrobe.

We had also taken as our own the ancient Christian sign of the Lamb and Cross and we embroidered it by hand on our dresses. The Lamb symbolises Jesus, the Lamb of God, and the cross is his call to follow him on that path. Only years later, when we began to examine our spiritual roots, did we realise that they were expressed in our emblem. The Lamb of God was beloved by the Moravians. Our spirituality could be traced through several strands that included the Evangelical Sisterhood of Mary, the Wesleys and the Moravians to the

Pietists, a Reform Movement in the Lutheran Church in Germany in the 17th century.

We were now quite near Wrexham. Sister Christine, the deaconess who had been friend and support for Lynda, was known to the two founding Sisters. The threads began to come together. On several occasions Christine brought the Youth Group from Wrexham to West Kirby. They joined in a day of teaching, sharing and singing in the still fledgling community, Sisters of Jesus Way. Lynda was one of the young people and so it came about that she met the community within which she was to find her life's work. The 13-year-old from Edinburgh was now a young woman trained as a nurse and midwife and had joined us. We were the four that were to stay together through joys, tribulations and sorrows until Lynda's early home-call. Later other Sisters joined, becoming very dear members of our family.

All this was in the future, although not so very far in the future for Lynda. She was 16 years old when we first met her. On her return to Wrexham she called at the office where her mother was working and told her that she wanted to join the Sisters of Jesus Way. Her mother was shocked and said immediately, "What about my grandchildren?" Lynda replied, "There are plenty of needy children in the world who need your love." The Sisters in West Kirby were blissfully unaware of this conversation. Lynda said nothing to us. Five years later she joined the community.

The Heavenly Father continued to prepare Lynda to be one of those who would form the foundation of the Sisters of Jesus Way. In two or three short years the Holy Spirit had transformed her life. Despite this, at college some of the old problems were surfacing as the time for A-Level examinations approached. A Sister in the community wrote to her, "I am very glad that you have decided not to worry about your grades." Whether Lynda was able to stick with this decision is doubtful but the Lord had healed her to the extent that she did not break down as had happened with her O-Level examinations. In a later letter from the same Sister comes the advice, "It really is more sensible to have a break and rest your mind."

We all have difficulties that are part of our make-up. Lynda, despite her smile and humour, tended to imagine the worst before it happened – and mostly it didn't happen. She tended to be more of a pessimist than an optimist. Deep-seated anxiety was a problem throughout her life and often this was in relation to illness. It wasn't only in exams that her over-conscientiousness and lack of confidence caused problems. It happened in other areas. One of our earliest recollections is a day when Lynda visited us. There was a large bowl of gooseberries that needed to be topped and tailed. We asked her if she would help us. She was glad to help, but filled with anxiety as to whether she was doing it correctly and whether there was time to finish the task. Almost anything there was to worry about a gooseberry she worried about that day. It was indicative as to where her battles were to be, as she grew in the Christian life. Fear, pride, perfectionism, self-condemnation – it was all there in this teenage girl alongside a gentle and caring nature. The Sister with whom she was corresponding wrote to Lynda with advice, "There is no (this is underlined twice) self-hatred in repentance." This was to be her battleground for many years.

She left Yale Sixth Form College on the 29th June 1982 and having passed her A-Levels with good grades, travelled to a new life at Hull University at the end of September 1982. She moved into Cleminson Hall (of residence). Methsoc (the Methodist Student Society) extended a welcome to her and there she made friends. She never warmed to it, as she had the youth group in Wrexham. The theology was more liberal and this was new to her. Deep within her she knew there was a different path, an intimate relationship with God. She had chosen to study German with French. Some of the literature that she had to read, especially the French, she found disturbing. The light she had glimpsed was a different light to that of the Enlightenment and humanist philosophy. A student who was on the same course and who kept in touch with Lynda through the years describes her as: "a very spiritual person", "mature" and "spiritually aware". In a letter to Lynda's parents this same friend wrote, "She was such a fundamentally good, kind, sympathetic person who displayed patience and sincerity in all aspects of her life."

Despite her inner doubts as to whether she was in the right place, she joined in with her friends – as one described it – "the giggles, the bad taste party, girls together against the books and exams". There were discussions about music and poetry. Moreover one of the men students fell in love with her. Was she to continue this relationship when there was within her a call which she couldn't clearly define but which she sensed would not be the way of marriage? There were many reasons that came together in her decision to leave Hull University after 18 months.

For Lynda the years before coming to the Sisters were years of preparation, but for the community also, they were a time of preparation for the work to which God had called us. On one thing we did not waver, and that was that our dependence for everything was on the Heavenly Father. Prayer was essential and built into the fabric and foundations of our life together. We wanted the furnishings in the house to be beautiful because the Lord Jesus was present with us. Beauty and a peaceful atmosphere go hand in hand. It wasn't so easy to bring this about when everything was second-hand or old furniture with new covers. It was a gift from God that soon all our different accessories blended together in perfect harmony. The semi-basement was made into a quiet chapel.

The Holy Spirit did not fail us but neither did the Heavenly Father spoil us. We tentatively started a ministry of hospitality. We refused to advertise, feeling that this was the thin end of the wedge as regards being a business. On our way of faith we trusted the Heavenly Father to send to us those in need of the shelter of our home. Gradually, by word of mouth, they came. The first year there were a hundred guests, most of whom we already knew. We turned away from anything that suggested that we did not trust the Heavenly

Father to provide for all our needs. We had become a Charitable Trust as that was the law of the land. That weighty document had been compiled when we were still in Manchester.

We learnt how to cook for larger numbers. There were some mishaps. If anything was to be a disaster with our newly acquired cooking skills it seemed to be the rice pudding. Once, we discovered too late that we had forgotten the key ingredient – rice. All we had was sweetened milk. Another time we hastily stood between our guests and the pudding when we spotted a baked potato that had fallen into it, unnoticed by us, while it was in the oven! Everything was done the hard way. We had no dryer, so sheets were all hung outside. They were washed in an old-fashioned washing machine where we had to do much of the work. Dishwashers were unknown. In addition we didn't have our own rooms and often had to move out to make way for guests.

The areas into which we had to venture where we had no previous knowledge were seemingly endless. This could be seen as one big adventure or a series of heart-stopping experiences depending on temperament. Accounting was another area where we were ignorant. None of us knew anything about bookkeeping and a balance sheet was incomprehensible. One day our doorbell rang and it was a retired Welsh Presbyterian minister, Glyn Holden, who had previously been an accountant. He taught us all we needed to know. The big ledger books were bought and entries were laboriously made. There were no computers with Excel making it easy! If Glyn had any doubts as to whether we would come unstuck financially on the path that we were on, he never expressed them. Plenty of others spoke out.

When we said that there were to be no set charges for a stay with us but a donation box for visitors to give what they could afford, our friends were appalled. They were convinced that we were heading for financial ruin. We were continually being urged to be business-like. It was a Roman Catholic priest who said to us, "You cannot rely on Providence too much." At the end of our first year it was Glyn that drew together the figures and presented a balance sheet. He said that if he had still been in business he would have said that it was a perfect balance sheet. We saw and still see the perfection of God in our finances.

Occasionally we were in a really tight spot. A lady who was staying with us had a short nap on our settee. She kicked off her shoes. Unnoticed by any of us, our labrador dog, seizing the opportunity, slunk furtively behind the settee with one of her shoes and gnawed his way through a substantial part of it before he was discovered. She was not surprisingly very upset, as they were a good pair of shoes. Miraculously, we had had some shoes given to us only a few days before that were the same colour, the right size and also a very good make. So we were able to replace her shoes immediately. The Heavenly Father thankfully answered before the prayer was even uttered.

There was sadness, too. In the short time that we lived in Lang Lane we looked after three people who were terminally ill. The father of one Sister and the aunt of another Sister spent their last months with us. A close friend also chose to die with us. Our GP gave us unstinting support. He was a devout Roman Catholic and understood community better than most. There were many areas where we were failing. The Lord was patient with us. We had not learnt to go the way of the Lamb with all our heart, as we did in later years. It was also difficult for the two founder Sisters to shed their deaconess mantles. It was a role they had had for many years. We were all learning in many areas.

Spiritually the emerging community and Lynda were moving in the same direction. We were all reading books written by, or about, Amy Carmichael of Dohnavur and Sister Eva of Friedenshort, women who had left all to follow Christ. With her excellent memory Lynda absorbed and remembered what she had read. They too had walked a way of faith, lived in community and had heard the call to leave all and follow Jesus out of love for him. They were also honest and wrote it as it really was, not clouded by piety or cloaking the difficulties.

Lynda was drawn to one book in particular, *A Foretaste of Heaven*, written by Mother Basilea Schlink. Mother Basilea was one of the founding Mothers of the Evangelical Sisterhood of Mary in Darmstadt, Germany. She wrote of a first love for Jesus. It was this that Lynda was seeking and so were the Sisters. We had travelled sufficiently far on our journey to know that this was not to be found in exalted mystical experiences or even the exuberance of Renewal Meetings, helpful though both may be at certain times in our lives. This love is grounded in the cross. Mother Basilea shared openly about her own difficulties and those of the Sisters in her community. For someone facing her own inner turmoil, as Lynda was, this was an encouragement. It gave her hope that there was a way through when she was tempted to fall into despair. For us also, it pointed to a way through our early travails.

The inner journey had begun for Lynda. It had begun for us also, as it must with everyone if there is to be growth in the Christian life. It is the way of sanctification or holiness, God's call to all who follow him. We were aware of this, but we needed help.

The Call

"We are called to love and honour the Lord Jesus Christ, friend of sinners, with a first love, a bridal love. 'I belong to my lover and his desire is for me.'"[1]

Some years later Lynda spoke about her call.

> At the age of fourteen I wrote in a diary I was keeping at that time, "I want to be a Bride of Jesus." I didn't understand what it meant. I wasn't even a Christian at the time but the Holy Spirit was at work in my heart even then.

In January 1984 she wrote to the Motherhouse of the Evangelical Sisterhood of Mary in Darmstadt in what was then West Germany, asking if they would accept her as a helper in the summer. The reply a week later was welcoming and all that Lynda sought. One of the Mary Sisters, Sister Divina wrote, "We have a small group of so-called, 'Canaan Helpers', who work with us for a short time and take part in our spiritual life." The letter ends, "Wishing you the Lord's guidance and His blessing, yours sincerely in His love." Lynda's heart was warmed. She arrived back in Wrexham from Hull and stayed with her parents. In the summer she travelled to Germany. The three months living on their little land of Canaan were formative.

Some of the Mary Sisters still remember her from that visit. They describe her as: "so very alive", with "a gentle spirit". She loved being alongside them and with other helpers. She delighted in the different nationalities and languages, the Bible studies, the beautiful worship and the talks she was able to have with various Sisters. Some of the practical work was a steep learning curve, especially with the exacting German standards. She forever after knew how to clean a washbasin using an old toothbrush! Spiritually she felt at home and found their emphasis on first love for Jesus echoing in her heart. This was her calling – to love Jesus exclusively. For much of her time on Canaan there was glorious sunshine and the sunshine of God's love shone in her heart. She returned to Wales, but only for a few months.

The little land of Canaan also had significance for the two founding Sisters of the Sisters of Jesus Way. It was while on retreat there, that one of them was given the name of the community and also the decision was made to take the Lamb and Cross as our emblem. Before they left, a bowl was passed around at the meal table. Everyone was invited to take a saying from it. One was, "Easy days, successful days, have never produced fruit of eternal worth. Only hard days do that." That was a bit daunting, although they had already seen the truth of what they read. The other was, "Learn to love the days of humble beginnings." That was a great encouragement.

Lynda had continued visiting us both before and after her visit to Germany. It was with us that she found a spiritual home. When, however, she said that she felt called to join us, she met opposition and discouragement from friends and family alike. Even her minister was against it. It was painful especially when Christian friends expressed their opposition. She began to experience in reality that first love for Jesus is also the way of the cross. It also revealed that underneath the gentle and shy exterior there was courage, determination and strength. Perhaps she had kept the letter from Sister Christine, written when she was 17 years old, so that she could read again those words, "Have courage to follow." A few weeks after her 21st birthday she answered what she believed to be a call from God and joined the Sisters. She knew us well and had seen our failures, as well as those places where the Heavenly Father was blessing us and caring for us. There was a steady, inner certainty that this was where she belonged. She wrote later:

Finding God's will for our lives should be a joyful experience of determining what adventure the Lord and we are going to engage in next.

There was something beautiful in giving Jesus her first love when she was in the springtime of her life. She commented 15 years later that she had been given a wonderful promise, just before she entered community, which she often recalled to mind.

"The Lord will guide you always; he will satisfy your needs in a sun-scorched land and will strengthen your frame. You will be like a well-watered garden, like a spring whose waters never fail."[2] And then we (I) will be able to give life to others, becoming a source of life, quenching the thirst of others. Our lives will no longer be sterile but will bear much fruit.

Lynda had not reached a sudden decision. Young though she was she had for years felt intuitively that this was the way for her and that losing her life, as the world saw it, was the way to life in all its fullness. This it proved to be. Many years later she gave this talk on "community". It is her credo for her own vocation and for that of each one who has heard a call to serve the Lord in the Sisters of Jesus Way.

A sign to the world
We are the most "me" generation ever and more attached to machines than to each other! A Christian community living together in love and forgiveness is a sign to the world. Indeed, as a snippet of our Rule of Life stipulates, "As we live together in love and forgiveness we witness to the kingdom of God. In a world of fragmented relationships others see the unity that only Christ can give. From our hidden lives comes peace to the troubled, light in the darkness and love for the stranger at the gate." The joyful admission that we need each other is not a sign of

weakness but of strength. "A community is not simply a group of people who live together and love each other. It is a place of resurrection, a current of life."[3]

Stability

Many people are restless and rootless. People are forced to move and establish themselves in new surroundings. Communities are fixed points and are a blessing. They offer that stability which St Benedict of Nursia writes about in his famous rule. A community that stays together for life can be a place of security for those who visit them. The guest can count on finding the same Brothers and Sisters, going through the same order of things every day. It is a place of stability also for those who live there if they are willing to face themselves in all their weaknesses and gradually make that transition from "the community for myself" to "myself for the community".[4]

Commitment

We live in a world where people shy away from commitment. We are frightened that if we put down roots in one soil we will curtail our freedom. It is true that if you marry one man or woman you give up millions of others – and that is a curtailment of freedom! But freedom doesn't grow in the abstract; it grows in a particular soil with a particular people. A community of people who are committed to one another is a sign to the world. There is freedom when we make a commitment to God and to each other. We become all that we are meant to be!

The formation of our community

When Lynda wrote these words she had proved them to be true in her own life. She goes on in her talk to speak of the particular community to which she had been called – The Sisters of Jesus Way. She writes:

There have been many strands that have been instrumental in the formation of our community but primarily these have been the gospels, the charismatic renewal and the lives of the saints of many denominations. There is a similarity with the Pietists of old – 17th-century Philipp Jakob Spener (the father of Pietism) and his successor, Auguste Hermann Francke, hymn writers Count Nikolas Ludwig von Zinzendorf, Paul Gerhardt and Joachim Neander. Their emphasis was personal holiness and personal devotion to Jesus, their practice of Christianity (faith expressing itself through love) rather than simply head knowledge. Sermons were to be understood, lead to repentance and encourage faith instead of being learned discourses! There was an overall joy and winsomeness about them.

She could have been speaking about her own life.

Our call

She continues,

> In a nutshell our emphases, as written in our Rule: "We are called to love and honour the Lord Jesus Christ, friend of sinners, with a first love, a bridal love . . . Jesus is our treasure. Our ministry of hospitality flows from this first calling – to love Jesus devotedly. We follow a way of faith, trusting our Heavenly Father to provide all our needs. We make our needs known only to him in prayer and therefore we don't ask for gifts or make known those needs outside the community. In this way we are able to give glory to God when our prayers are answered.
>
> Prayer, either using the framework of a simple liturgy, or informal, is central to all that we do. We make life promises of simplicity, fidelity and chastity. Our work for the Lord varies as the Holy Spirit opens and closes doors."[5]

Early Years in Community

"There is no need too small that we cannot take it to our Heavenly Father or any need too large that we cannot trust him to provide. Again and again he surprises us with his goodness."

Lynda ends her talk (her credo) by saying, "Sister Hazel will now share the exciting story of our beginnings!" "Exciting" it certainly was and many other things besides. The community, Sisters of Jesus Way, was barely five years old and still being formed when Lynda began her journey with us. This quiet, reserved girl was now destined to play an important role, as the nest where many would find shelter in coming years, was built. None of us guessed the gifts that lay behind the quiet exterior. She was equally unaware of them herself. She had a disconcerting way of saying "I can't" before any new challenge. As we learnt to ignore this protestation we discovered that when she did what she said she couldn't do, she invariably did it with great competence and giftedness.

About the time Lynda joined us our sojourn at Lang Lane came to an end, quite suddenly and unexpectedly. Our visitors had increased in number year on year. We were moving bedrooms frequently in order to fit everyone in. Our ingenuity for doing the near impossible and accommodating guests in an already overcrowded house was fast running out. One day we had to refuse a minister in need. We knew something had to be done. We studied the house closely. There was a possibility that we could divide three rooms but once that was accomplished there was no way that we could expand any further. We made enquiries and were told that the cost would be about six thousand pounds. Our gifts had unexpectedly increased and we wondered if that was the reason. We were uneasy spending that amount of money knowing that it could only be a temporary measure. There did not seem to be an alternative.

We decided to go ahead and trust that the Lord would close the door if we were making a mistake. We asked three builders to give us estimates for the work. Before we received the third estimate the door closed, or it would be more accurate to say a door opened. The telephone rang during our evening prayers. An elderly lady, Mrs Elsie Porter, had died, leaving her house to charity. One of the trustees was her son, J. Mason Porter and he very much wanted us to be that charity. We knew the house, as we had visited Mrs Porter, a gracious and generous Christian lady. It was called Redacre, a large and beautiful house in an acre of land. There was a sense of awe at the Father's perfect timing.

Everything was changing as Lynda moved in. She was not by nature a pioneer or one who sought constant activity but this was precisely the situation she encountered. It was no easy, gentle entry into a community. From the first she shouldered responsibilities and took part in the decision-making. We would now endeavour to protect younger Sisters from such an admission to our midst. Wherever our heart lay, it was impossible to protect her. Perhaps the Heavenly Father had to look after this child in a special way.

She also had the privilege of learning valuable lessons, especially in the area of prayer, as we encountered many difficulties. Redacre is situated in what is euphemistically called a "sensitive area" and so we were not certain that the neighbours would welcome us. Some were grateful, as, if nothing else, we were not property developers. Despite all this there were objections. For Lynda, there was an early introduction to the truth of the words of Jesus, "Woe to you when all men speak well of you."[1] We prayed about everything – especially the problems that came our way. We saw mountains become smooth places.

Lynda was one of the Sisters who moved in first ("camped in the house" would be a better expression). On 1st February 1985 we all moved in. Our arrival at Redacre was very different from our light-hearted arrival at Lang Lane. Even the weather seemed to echo the difference. It was cold, and despite normally warm winters on the Wirral, February 1985 proved to be the exception with snow on the ground some six inches deep within days. Nora Porter fell in the kitchen and broke her wrist when she was helping us. Circumstances began to take their toll. We were still grieving the loss of family members. Our concerned doctor drove one of the Sisters, who had sustained the most recent loss, to the Lake District. Here a deaconess, Sister Constance, who had come alongside us and was our official visitor, welcomed her to her home in Ambleside. Those of us who were left succumbed to flu.

Storage heaters had warmed the house but these had partly been dismantled as the work on installing central heating began. We lit fires in the open grates, but as soon as we vacated these rooms, wintry blasts from outside swirled around through doors left open by workmen. Any exposed parts felt in danger of frostbite! Lynda sat shivering in front of a coal fire in her Laura Ashley dress plus woolly hat and scarf. She persevered.

We discovered water seeping through the parquet floor of the basement. It did not seem serious but nevertheless needed investigation. To our dismay we discovered that the house was sinking at one end. The cause was an underground stream. We thought wryly again of the promise we had received from Deuteronomy, "A land of brooks of water, of fountains and springs."[2] The brook was right underneath the house and had been washing away the sand on which it was built, for years. As the house sank, drainage pipes fractured, so we were awash with water. The brook was diverted and the house had to be underpinned. Naturally our insurers would not have paid, as we had so recently moved in and we had not had a surveyor, in retrospect a big mistake. Again the Lord was merciful. Mrs Porter's insurance had one more week to run and that company paid two thirds of the cost. We thanked the Lord again for his timing.

Within a few months we closed the house to visitors and builders began extensive alterations. Fire precautions and the need to divide rooms to make more single bedrooms made this work necessary. There was dust everywhere as walls were stripped bare, knocked down, or rebuilt. White sheets covered the beautiful furniture that we had inherited and footsteps echoed on bare floorboards. A mysterious bell kept ringing and although we rushed to the back and front doors there was no one there. It was much later that we discovered that it was the old bell that was used to summon the maid and the wires were touching in the loft. We could not afford double-glazing for the windows so in DIY mode we Sellotaped polythene across the panes. At night a ghostly organ began playing. It was some time before we realised that the wind was providing a concert for us, as it rippled between the polythene and the glass.

The garden had once been well designed but it had become overgrown. As spring arrived everything sprang into life, including the weeds. High privet hedges that were already unruly threatened to take over. We didn't even own a hedge-cutter. It was unending. So was the list of new equipment we had to buy. We left the dahlias in the ground because we didn't have time to lift them. They had been a brilliant display in the autumn, the only flowerbed that had been tended in the whole garden. We had an exceptionally hard frost and lost them all. It was the garden that brought us to the edge of despair. How were we going to keep on top of it?

There was some compensation. We discovered an ancient path that we saw on the deeds of the house and had been in existence before the land was bought. It was originally called the Beech Walk. The ancient beech trees still shaded it and in the spring bluebells carpeted the edges. The more imaginative amongst us wondered who had walked there in days long past. We later renamed this path, the Praise Path; praising the Heavenly Father who had brought us to this beautiful land. We could see the tides as they ebbed and flowed in the Dee Estuary, and beyond that, the Welsh mountains. On clear days Snowdon edged the skyline. Lynda loved beauty and the estuary was dear to her all her life, the sun glinting on the water, the sunsets over the sea reflecting gold, orange, pink, the call of the wild birds.

Much later we discovered that the house was built on what had once, many centuries ago, been monastic land. Cistercian monks from Holywell had rowed across the Dee Estuary in their small boats and farmed our land. There was a sense of tranquillity even in our overgrown garden and a neighbour spoke to us about the peace she felt on her property. The saints leave their mark; the impression of their footsteps can last for centuries. We had a strange sense that in some way we had come home. In our own small way we are part of the monastic tradition, albeit in 21st-century guise, and we felt rooted in the Christian past. We didn't have much time for such musings! As well as the amount of work, our finances kept us focussed.

We lived by prayer. A way of faith, or trust in the Heavenly Father, does not always protect from anxiety. There were many times that we were worried but we remained faithful to our calling. We made no appeals for money and mentioned our needs to no one. We prayed fervently. The end of our financial year was 31st August. In just seven months we had spent £41,386 and that was on top of our ordinary running expenses, which were considerably higher than for the house in Lang Lane. This was to rise to £77,235 before Redacre was fully functional for our use. The sums were staggering. Instead of dealing in hundreds of pounds, which had been our experience at Lang Lane, we were now dealing in thousands. We had no idea before we moved of the costs we would be facing. In addition to this our domestic equipment did not cope with the extra work and we had to invest several thousand pounds on such items as a commercial dishwasher, washing machine and dryer. Yet miraculously, as each bill came, we were able to pay. We never went into debt. The Heavenly Father provided.

Redacre was built solidly, as many of our workmen discovered to their cost as they tried to drill into walls and floors. It is sturdy and strong, able to withstand the fiercest of storms rolling in from the Irish Sea. It reminded us of the security we find in our Heavenly Father, who is strong and able to protect in all the storms of life.

Never the most robust physically, Lynda lived through these days working and praying. She showed the inner strength that we had seen when she first answered the call to join us. We can't remember her grumbling, at least not any more than the rest of us! One day Sister Connie warned us about grumbling. It must have been prevalent. It wasn't only the finance but all the work. We knew too, that the sin of grumbling must stop or the Heavenly Father's provision for us would cease. We had read what happened to the children of Israel in the wilderness when they grumbled. Some days everything was quite overwhelming. The antidote to grumbling is thanksgiving. We had been placed in a hard school of spiritual discipline.

Lynda experienced these anxious days but also saw the Heavenly Father in miraculous ways take care of his little flock. She never hesitated, after that experience, in witnessing to the way of faith to which she had been called and delighted through the years in telling the story of our move to Redacre and the many answers to prayer that she saw. We will forever be grateful for her faithfulness through those difficult years. Fidelity is now one of the promises we make at our Bridal Consecration. Lynda, so young and new in community, was living it even then. "Fidelity is faithfulness to God and to each other, especially when the going is tough."3

We made a small upstairs room into a beautiful chapel. Through the window we could see leafy trees in summer, while in winter delicate dark branches wove patterns swaying in the wind. It was an oasis of peace. An established pattern of daily prayer gave stability in an otherwise chaotic time. After a few months when there was some semblance of order, a service was held in our chapel and Lynda wore her blue dress for the first time. She loved our dress and never expressed any desire to be wearing the latest fashions as most of her contemporaries were. One day, in Birkenhead, accompanied by another Sister, a stranger walked up to them and said, "You look beautiful and happy, too." She did, wherever she went.

We were a community still in formation in Lynda's early years and this brought challenges for all of us but she was happy. A former neighbour emailed us,

> She always had such a willing smile and greeting. I called her "the new girl", because she was, when I lived next door. I didn't know her name, but she did make an impact. She was always smiling when I met her or saw her.

A former friend from university days met Lynda again at a wedding and wrote,

> I clearly remember seeing the new peace in her eyes, the peace of someone who had found home.

The Inner Journey

"Break free from the culture of blaming others and instead acknowledge your own faults. 'The sacrifices of God are a broken spirit; a broken and contrite heart, O God, you will not despise.'"[1]

"The ego with all its demands, the 'I wants', the touchiness, petty jealousies, resentments, pride and self-righteousness must die. 'If anyone would come after me, he must deny himself and take up his cross and follow me. For whoever wants to save his life will lose it, but whoever loses his life for me will find it.'"[2]

Sister Eulalia, a Sister from the Evangelical Sisterhood of Mary, stayed with us for a short time when we were still living in Lang Lane. She gave a word of prophecy during our morning prayers. She spoke of the many difficulties that we would face from within the community, but we were not to be dismayed because we were enclosed in the tent of God's love. The difficulties were there, but more importantly so was the tent of God's love. Although it wasn't obvious to others, our greatest difficulties were, as this word from the Lord said, "within". We had been warned about relationships before we started – this causes the shipwreck of many communities, as it does of many team ministries. One community seriously warned us against founding a community because of the difficulties in relationships. We were aware of the problem but we couldn't see a way through.

From the beginning individual Sisters and occasionally Brothers from other communities drew alongside us and we learnt from them. Especially dear to us was Sister Florence, a Sister from Our Lady of Evron, a Roman Catholic Order. One day the doorbell rang and a frail, elderly nun stood on the doorstep. We invited her in. When she saw our large dog she was so afraid that she almost faded into the wall. However she had come to meet us and meet us she was determined to do. Her friendship meant much to us through the years. One of her sayings that always remained dear to us was, "Always say 'yes' to the will of God even when you say it in tears." When the dark valleys have come we have clung to that advice.

Also in our early days we answered the door one day and saw a man whom we thought, at first, was a tramp. Then we spotted a brown habit peeping out from a raincoat that had seen better days. He was an Anglican Franciscan Brother. Somewhere he had heard about us and had come to see what was happening. Brother Ronald crossed our path a number of times and always encouraged us. His emphasis was praise. As he stood in our path one day some slates fell from the roof. Our thoughts were, "Oh dear, more expense," but before we had time to say anything, he hesitated slightly and said, "Praise the Lord, anyway." That was Brother Ronald!

Lynda was blessed in joining this rich tapestry of friendships from other communities. We were encouraged that they had sought us out. It was a Sister from the Evangelical Sisterhood of Mary who eventually came to our rescue over relationships. This was the community where Lynda had been a helper and the two founder Sisters had spent time in retreat. Years before, we had been impressed, as we felt they had found a way through on relationships.

As the Heavenly Father had provided for us materially he now proceeded to do so spiritually. The two founder Sisters were still at that time deaconesses and were obliged to go to a Convocation lasting a few days. It was being held in London Colney. They arrived there rather battered by recent events in the community and not too happy at having to leave home. A Sister had left after months of being unsettled. It was not a good leaving. They felt that for the sake of a still fragile community, as she was still in the area, the separation must be clear and definite now that she had made the decision.

They lacked the courage to do it, knowing that they would be misunderstood.

While in London Colney they realised that Radlett was only a few miles away. The Mary Sisters had their English branch in this small town. They knew one of the Sisters. One afternoon they decided to visit her. They rang the bell at Jesus' Return, the name of the branch house, and were rather taken aback when it was not the Sister they knew but one that they didn't know who came to the door. Moreover, she was German and had only come to the UK recently. She was aware that her English was not as good as she would have liked it to be. That may be, but by the time they left, they fully understood all she was saying. Their first surprise was when she said that she was praying for a community on the Wirral. They didn't need to share their difficulties or cover them up. She already knew them. Furthermore she had every intention of addressing them and helping. This she did. She understood, coming from a community, the difficulties they were in. She gave wise advice and the courage to do what they had known in their hearts was right.

The Heavenly Father is faithful. Although they did not realise it they were meeting the Sister who, in the future, we were all to love dearly, and she us. Moreover she was Sister Divina, who had answered Lynda's request to go to Canaan in Darmstadt some years before. In the Joseph stories in the book of Genesis, Joseph says to his brothers who had plotted against him, "You intended to harm me but God intended it for good."[3] This was now our experience. Criticism against us had been used by God to bring the help that we needed. Only our loving Heavenly Father could have cared for us in such a way. He wounds in order to heal. The visit that day was the turning point in our community life.

After they returned home we all talked together. We wondered whether this Mary Sister would come and lead a few days' retreat. We hesitated to even ask but eventually took our courage in both hands and contacted her. It was here that we saw the generosity of the Evangelical Sisterhood of Mary and the self-giving of this particular Sister who was a stranger in a strange land and at an age when she should possibly have been thinking of an easier life. To our delight she agreed to visit us. She told us later that she was drawn to us because she saw in us a first love for Jesus, but she also saw the places where we needed help and felt sorry for us! Sister Divina arrived in West Kirby. That was the beginning of a breakthrough in our relationships.

The inner journey is our relationship with the Lord in the secret places of our hearts; it is facing the sin within and finding forgiveness and redemption. For every Sister living in community this journey must take place and that alone in the end is the answer to difficult relationships. It is a journey into Love and learning to love not in words only but from the heart. It can only, ". . . be a place of stability," as Lynda wrote in her credo, "if we are willing to face our weaknesses," and "gradually make the transition from 'the community for myself' to 'myself for the community'." "Myself for the community" sounds deceptively easy but it is a life of sacrifice, death to the ego, and the way of the cross.

We felt that if we could only understand each other and indeed understand ourselves, we would emerge better Christians. We are not saying that self-knowledge is a bad thing but it can be the enemy of the best. We underestimated – if not outrightly ignored – the fact, which is clear throughout Scripture, that we are sinners. Where was the gospel that the founder Sisters had so confidently proclaimed in their caravan missions? It wasn't there. They had lost sight of it and were badly off centre. Psychology may have its place but it is a subservient place to the gospel. We didn't see it but we were bound by the greatest sin of all, self-righteousness. Self-righteousness makes us spiritually blind. It keeps every other sin in place. We needed someone else to show us this, to break through our pride and point us back to the saving power of Christ.

Community living is a great grace because with our different personalities, temperaments and faults it isn't long before our sinful nature begins to show, sometimes quite spectacularly – pride, self-pity, touchiness, impatience, irritability, jealousy and so on. We acknowledged we were sinners but we were not keen on the specific, that is, where we were sinning and naming the sin. When we overcame that hurdle, as we could hardly deny our faults, we were equally good in the next breath at excusing ourselves. An example would be that someone was impatient and irritable but that Sister would then reason, "I would not have been like that if Sister X had not been slow and difficult!" Another then began to feel resentful but was certain that she would not have been if Sister Y had not been thoughtless. It continued, excuse after excuse, continually justifying ourselves. We were taught one simple lesson: to put a full stop after the "but".

There were many other excuses that came tumbling out. It is my temperament, my past, my ill health. We were told, "No excuses!" When we start to justify ourselves we are closing the door to God's grace because we are not admitting our need. We were taught afresh the path of repentance. Jesus described himself as the Good Physician. If we take the medicine that we are sinners then we are within sight of the healing. Or to put it another way – when we know our need and turn in humble contrition then the Lord is waiting for us. This is the gospel. Suddenly we had hope. Along this path, the Lord Jesus who had died for us could and would change us. He did not do it in the twinkling of an eye but over the years, his grace drew us ever closer to himself. We saw in each other a miracle of grace as old attitudes began to fall away. This is not to say that we became perfect! We knew, however, where there was help to be found.

We slowly became compassionate instead of condemning, and learnt to give space to a struggling Sister. We were no longer drawn into each other's sin. The latter was a breakthrough for us because until we had the help in seeing, sin was begetting sin in the community. For example, Sister X was in a bad mood, a black cloud hovered about her; Sister Y, who had been quite happy, found herself becoming resentful at this intrusion into her good spirits, while Sister Z, viewing the scene, judged them both and fell into self-righteousness. Add self-pity to that and it is a potent mix! We learnt to put the cross or the blood of Jesus between the one who was struggling and ourselves, pray for them and bless them in Jesus' name.

Lynda was privileged in learning these lessons while she was still young, but at the same time they created a problem, or rather revealed a problem that was already there. Lynda, who had learnt to trust the love of God in material things, as she became more aware of her own sin and failings, found it difficult to do the same spiritually. Again and again the question came to her:

> Can Jesus really love me? Time and time again I believe that God has had enough because I am falling into the same sins and that he cannot love me. I hardly dare believe that his love for me is without end.

Many were the hours spent by those who were alongside her on her journey helping her through this. The truth is that the Lord loves sinners, it is our self-righteous self that does not. It is a blessed moment when we realise that we truly are sinners and there is forgiveness and healing through the cross of the Lord Jesus.

Through the grace, mercy and faithfulness of God, the spiritual foundations of the community were secured. The four of us who were together at that first visit by Sister Divina were still together, although with other Sisters by then, until the day the Lord called Lynda home. We were not an easy four, very different in temperament, but his grace is sufficient. "As we live together in love and forgiveness we witness to the Kingdom of God. In a world of fragmented relationships, others see the unity that only Christ can give."[4]

Sometimes we are put on a pedestal, although hopefully not by those who know us best. Lynda, who was in many ways such an attractive person, found that this could easily happen to her. She would laugh if anyone had such false notions. Those who love us best are those who love us knowing all our faults and failures. That love she found in Christ and in her Sisters. We learn more through our weaknesses than our strengths. They bring us to a deeper dependence on the Lord and help us to grow in humility. It was Lynda's journey on this pathway that later gave her discernment both with Sisters and guests, enabling her to give wise and understanding advice.

She made into a prayer for herself, a poem that she found written in a guest book on one of her visits to Canaan in Darmstadt. It may have been written in German and Lynda translated it or it may have been in English.

Deep in me Lord, mark Thou Thy holy cross,
On choices, private dear desires, and motives.
Let all that self in any form inspires
Be unto me as dross.
When the touch of death is here and there
Laid on a thing most precious in my eyes,
Let me recognise the answer to my prayer.[5]

Bridal Consecration

"Bridal love pours out the 'alabaster jar of very expensive perfume'.[1] *It does not count the cost but seeks only to comfort the Lord in his suffering."*

Two years before Lynda's Bridal Consecration the words, "'I know the thoughts that I think toward you,' saith the Lord, 'thoughts of peace, and not of evil, to give you an expected end',"[2] came to her attention. She was only 25 years old but she wrote,

> "An expected end" . . . means that Jesus will mould me . . . to be like him, that I might see him and share his glory.

Then she added the comment, "I can't wait."

Before she became a Sister of Jesus Way, Lynda counted the cost. Her great love was foreign languages, especially German, and as far as she could see she was joining an English speaking community with English speaking visitors and there would be no opportunity to speak anything other than English. This was a sacrifice for her. Anticipating this, she had surrendered her will to God's will on this matter before she came to join us. Within a short time, however, it became apparent that we needed a German speaker. One Swiss German helper proved to be the first of many, and visitors came, as well, especially from Switzerland and Germany. German rapidly became the second language in the community. Lynda's giftedness in languages was not restricted to German. She enjoyed meeting guests from other countries and amazed us when after one meeting she would speak sentences in Swahili, Chinese or some other language.

She had also given to the Lord her desire to travel. We found that as we gave hospitality here then our friends from

Germany and Switzerland wanted to reciprocate the kindness. Links were renewed with the Evangelical Sisterhood of Mary and we travelled to their retreats in Germany. Lynda was our interpreter. It has always been our desire that each Sister should once in her lifetime visit Israel. It is expensive. When we were unexpectedly given a gift enabling two Sisters to go to the Holy Land, Lynda was one of the Sisters. The wonder of her stay in Israel never left her. She referred to the time spent there many times in Bible studies that she gave. One of her last breaks was in Sardinia, where friends had lent us their villa. With phrase book firmly in hand, she returned home with a fair grasp of Italian.

She commented many times that the sacrifices she had made to the Lord he had returned to her a hundredfold.

Early in the morning of 23rd February 1991, the Sisters met together in the little chapel in Redacre. The ring that later that day would be placed on Sister Lynda's finger was blessed. Sister Divina, who Lynda had first met eight years before on Canaan in Darmstadt, prayed over the ring, "We thank you, Lord Jesus, that just as this ring has no ending so it is with your love, your everlasting grace and mercy."

In the afternoon Lynda's parents and a few friends, including our neighbour Hilary, joined us. It was Sister Lynda's service of Bridal Consecration and she was radiant. We were few in number as the chapel was quite small. It did not matter. Those she loved and who loved her were there. A friend, Rev. Keith Knight, a Methodist minister, led the service. She made her promises to the Lord – simplicity, fidelity and chastity.

She spoke in the service,

It is truly the happiest day of my life. I may be very nervous, shaking like a leaf, but I am very happy. In many ways it is the equivalent of a wedding day, but yet it is far more than that. I know we can't hear wedding bells but I feel sure that they are ringing in heaven. I sense too that some of the angels have spilled out of heaven to share my joy.

It is the happiest day of my life because it marks the beginning of the fulfilment of my longing to be a Bride of Jesus, to be near him always, to be loved by him and to love him. Today marks his "yes" to me, and my "yes" to him before earth and heaven. I thank him with all my heart that he has placed me in this community with my Sisters to love him as his bride. My deepest desire today is that this day would bring joy to Jesus, that there would be a song of joy in his heart. The world is so dark. May he be comforted today. The love of Jesus shines like the sun. He is the light of the world. I want to give him everything; I want to give him my life.

In the evening there was a Festival. Lynda comments,

We didn't half sing! . . . good practice for heaven . . . where voices inexhaustible will be granted.

She records a message from one of the angels who spilled out of heaven to survey the event. We are not sure which human hand gave her this message but it echoes now in our hearts for her, "Heaven – where we will receive the kiss of God." Inside the little gold crown she received that day were the words, "Who will live in heaven's glory? – Those who hasten day by day towards the goal above."[3]

She knew realistically that there is no easy path to heaven. We travel to heaven over the rough plains of earth. At the time of her Bridal Consecration she wrote down, "Words of Scripture to cherish":

For he (God) himself has said, I will not in any way fail you nor give you up nor leave you without support. I will not, I will not, I will not in any degree leave you helpless, nor forsake you, nor let you down, relax my hold on you –

Assuredly not! So we take comfort and are encouraged and confidently and boldly say, The Lord is my helper . . .[4]

For thus it stands in scripture: Behold I am laying in Zion a chosen, (honoured) precious chief cornerstone; and he who believes in him – who adheres to, trusts in and relies on him – shall never be disappointed or put to shame.[5]

The joy of her Bridal Consecration never left her and each year on 23rd February she looked back and remembered,

> I wish to thank you, my Lord Jesus, for your "almost tangible" peace in my heart today – in an extremely busy day – a special gift on the anniversary of my Bridal Consecration (16 years ago)! My heart was deeply moved when we sang about you in our morning prayer – "The One who with a powerful word stilled the sea, yet silently you suffered for my sake, for love of me."[6] Thank you for your faithful love in my moments of unfaithfulness, my dearest Lord Jesus!

Her 20th anniversary was to be her last. There is a note in her diary –

> 20 years ago I made my Bridal Consecration – giving my "yes" to Jesus to be His Bride. Many times I have been so unfaithful but he has overflowed in his faithfulness towards me. Polycarp's Day . . . too – I felt his fatherly smile upon me.

In 1991, the year of Lynda's Bridal Consecration, we decided that we would take new names. These are now given during a clothing service, as life in the community begins for a new Sister. Rather than abandon completely our name from birth, which we felt for us would not be appropriate, we chose instead to put after our name descriptive words that would remind us of our calling. A Sister who struggled with pride chose, "of the humble Saviour", another who tended to legalism, "of the Lord of grace" and another chose, "of the gentle Lion of Judah". Lynda, with her difficulties in believing that the Lord could love her unless she was good, chose as her new name, "Sister Lynda of the Compassionate Face of Jesus." A card was given to each of us with a little commentary on it. The words that were given to Lynda were, "This name will call you to look often at the compassionate face of Jesus and to see there his love for you. He has compassion on the falls and the faults because he knows that in your heart you love and follow him. Looking at his face and at his love will enable you to be as compassionate with others as he is with you."

For Lynda it had been a momentous year.

Bethany

"We do not take for granted the love that surrounds us or the many gifts bestowed on us by the Heavenly Father. Those who live simply are always thankful."

In many ways, by autumn 1992, we felt that we had reached the end of our beginning. Some of our dear friends who had stood closely with us – Walter Walls, our first solicitor, Glyn Holden, our accountant, and Sister Florence, our much loved Roman Catholic Sister – had completed their pilgrimage and were in heaven. The two Sisters who had been Methodist deaconesses had resigned from that order with the blessing of the Rev. Brian Galliers, now on our Trust and formerly Warden of the Order, as well as that of our Methodist Chairman of the District, Rev. Dr John Newton. We knew that the Methodist Diaconal Order and the Sisters of Jesus Way must now travel their separate ways. They are two different callings.

Most traumatic for us all, including Lynda, was Sister Divina returning to her Motherhouse in Germany. We had not spent a great deal of time with her each year but Radlett seemed near and Darmstadt a long way away. It was a sorrowful parting. The Lord gave us a word from Daily Light, "I will not leave you as orphans; I will come to you."[1] It was a reassuring word for the remainder of our journey. What he promised, he has done, always guiding us and leading us forward. The contact was not lost, as we feared, since we travelled from time to time to Darmstadt. Some of us, including Lynda, treasured and kept letters that she wrote to us.

We had proved the faithfulness of God, giving us good friends, helpers and those who were able to assist us on our spiritual journey. Our material needs had always been met.

We were grateful. We started a thanksgiving evening once a week with our guests where we sang and praised God. This has continued latterly in our private community prayers. Every week we name the blessings we have received, and thank the Heavenly Father. There is always a long list.

The previous year we had started to build Bethany. Once again we were in difficulty over accommodation. We were living in Redacre and sharing the house with our guests. We firmly believed the community would grow. There would be a limit as to how long this arrangement would be feasible. The number of visitors was growing. There was the added difficulty that we had no "family" life together and sometimes were just that little bit too accessible. We looked at various possibilities but were advised that it would be cheaper to build a house than try and extend Redacre. We have always relied quite heavily on words, or a word, from Scripture to give us impetus in a situation. The word came, "They shall build houses and inhabit them . . . and my chosen shall long enjoy the work of their hands."[2] This seemed to be quite clear; we were to build this house ourselves.

There was also an inner certainty, a gift of faith given by the Lord, that this was the way forward. Some of our friends were again dismayed. Where was the money coming from? One dear friend put it gently, "We were concerned about the possible financial implications!" That was an understatement. Others didn't put it quite as gently! We were concerned, too, about the finance but we had learnt that when the Lord directs, then the safest path is to follow even if it does look, humanly speaking, impossible.

There were many other concerns. We didn't know how to build a house, not even how to mix cement. We tried to remedy some of our lack of knowledge by going around building sites and observing builders at work. Lynda was still a young Sister when these momentous decisions were made but she was very much part of the decision-making, and whatever it was going to cost us in sacrifice, prayer and hard

work, she was prepared to do it. We prayed much in words
and song:

Lord, we believe a house will stand
On our little bit of land.

And it will to your glory be
That our neighbours your power will see.

And so we thank you Lord today
That you have led us in this way.

And Lord your riches don't run dry,
For you will every need supply.

And for our architect we pray
That you will guide his hand today.

And for a builder Lord we pray
That the right one will come our way.

And joyful Sisters we will see
In the house that is to be.

The poetry wasn't brilliant, neither was the tune, but
interspersed with numerous hallelujahs and waving our
banners, our prayers reached up to heaven and encouraged
our faith.

An Egyptian Christian, who one of our Sisters met in
Germany, encouraged us. He said, "It will happen step by
step." We acted quite literally on this word. An architect who
understood our way of faith came alongside us. Plans were
drawn. We were given planning permission. There was
sufficient money for the foundations. We didn't look any
further than that. The day arrived, and a JCB trundled down
a ramp into the garden. Our neighbours looked on in shock,
as Lynda drove a dumper truck and another Sister guided the
JCB driver showing him where to dig. Later, Sisters in white
protective clothing hung on to the heavy nozzle as liquid

concrete was poured into the trenches. The story is told in full elsewhere.[3]

The foundations had been filled with quarry stone and sand. We rang the plant hire firm for a vibrator plate to compress them. The voice at the other end of the phone said, "You mean a whacker, who is it for?" The Sister replied, "The Sisters of Jesus Way." "Do you realise this whacker can whack you over the moon?" came the retort. They trusted us and allowed us to hire it.

We started the foundations with £20,836 and in a short time spent £20,673.13. Financially, this was the story throughout; we usually had enough money to do the next stage when we came to it but never enough to complete the house. If we didn't have the finance we stopped until we did. It was trust all the way. In some ways, Lynda had become so used to living this way that she accepted it quite easily. She had many concerns but finance was not one of them. She knew her Heavenly Father and his promises.

Although it wasn't a clear demarcation line, two worked on the building and two in Redacre. Both were difficult assignments. Lynda with another Sister took responsibility for Redacre. That one sentence encapsulates much hard work: cooking, cleaning, laundry, bed-making, answering the phone and the door, accounts, making visitors welcome, the list was endless. Helping in the kitchen gave her valuable experience. She was very particular about cleanliness. She was cheerful. One visitor remembers hearing her sing as she cleaned the loos. Her love of beauty came to the fore as she began to flower-arrange.

She welcomed visitors, keeping an unobtrusive eye on their needs. Moreover, working in Redacre, the sacrifices were not so obvious. This is a good place to be spiritually, but not easy. It was very obvious on the building site where Sisters were tackling jobs far beyond their expertise and strength. One way or another, however, we were all involved. Many and varied were her tasks and the days flew by – no two days were alike. The "I can't" was laid to rest and a gifted Sister emerged.

Her work was not divorced from her life in Christ. She was quick to acknowledge the Lord speaking to her through practical problems. One day, to her intense frustration, a letter she had written became locked in a word processor. We tried everything to no avail. Then the Lord spoke to her. She saw herself in the word processor. There was a natural reserve in her nature that made it tempting to lock failings and sins inside with no way out. She repented of this. The word processor sprang into action and the letter was retrieved.

The Lord had also spoken to us through the foundations of Bethany. The work that had been done could be viewed from an upstairs window in Redacre. It was a visitor who one day pointed out the cross to us. As the foundations had been built up, one layer consisted of damp proof membrane, blue polythene not unlike the blue of our dresses. Bricks marked out the rooms and these were filled with concrete leaving the remainder of the house area still to be brought up to floor level. As we looked down we could see a perfect blue cross stretching from end to end and side to side. Bethany was built over this cross. We knew that the Lord was saying that the cross must be in our hearts and in the foundation of our community life.

When the cross has come to us, and it came not long after, we knew that it was a call to a deeper dying and a deeper abandonment to the will of God. Lynda herself recalls this time:

> We cast ourselves on God, as never before. He drew near to us in his mercy and he spared the life of a Sister who had been diagnosed with cancer and with her the life of the community. This drawing near to God is one of the hidden treasures that emerge from the storms. Also in the storms our hearts are laid bare for what they are. "It is there in the storm that we discover the imperfections of our souls. While we are in other places which are pleasant, they hide themselves, and remain with us: but there in the

storm they, these imperfections, break out and show themselves!"[4]

The Lord brought us through. Lynda was still in her twenties.

Our serving the Lord is anchored in our worship of him. Before Bethany was completed we began building a chapel. The little room we had used for this purpose in Redacre was too small for our needs. It was a highlight when we celebrated our first communion in our Chapel of Adoration. Rev. Brian Galliers, our friend and mentor for many years, was the minister who presided. It was a beautiful summer's evening. The chapel was only half-built and had neither roof nor windows. The birds joined our praises; their notes clear in the evening air. Years before, our Heavenly Father had promised that just as he fed the birds of the air he would care for us. This he had done.

When it came to the outside painting of Bethany, Lynda came into her own. Along with another Sister she scaled the roof of our new house. She wrote her thoughts on this for our book,[5] from which the following excerpt has been taken:

I am very grateful to the Heavenly Father for his protection during the building period, for most afternoons and an occasional morning found me high and lifted up on the scaffolding, painting the wooden fascia boards which surround the edges of Bethany's roof. I am also thankful for the Father's gift of strength, as I made my way up and down the appointed apparatus in monkey-like fashion, and for the sense of satisfaction derived from seeing the dull grey undercoat give way to the rich Burgundy, which now adorns Bethany's gable end and roof edges.

But there was no greater joy to be compared with my stint/stunt, whichever way you would like to read it, on the roof itself during a few unusually glorious days in October. Due to the unusual shape of the house some painting work was necessary on fascias that could only be reached by ascending the middle portion of the roof.

I shall never forget my first ascent, or the subsequent ones for that matter. Our builder-friend had erected a roof ladder, which in turn was attached to the scaffolding. Having climbed up safely I turned myself around on my back ready to paint. A magnificent panorama stretched out before my eyes, the views were breath-taking. The Snowdonian range dominated the blue horizon with its snow-capped peaks. The familiar forms of the Great and Little Ormes and the nearer Welsh hills were vividly clear in the autumn sunshine. A few ships seemed to greet me, as they journeyed the Irish Sea. I completely forgot the painting for some minutes, as I gazed at God's wonderful creation, revelled in it and received it as a love-gift from my Heavenly Father.

The following few days the praise times continued in this unlikely spot high up on Bethany's roof. There was even enough time to do the painting too.

She had no fear of heights. She shouted down to us about the wonderful view. Our hearts were in our mouths. Those of us on the ground were the ones who were afraid. She was too agile to fall. The painting was successfully completed and the two Sisters returned to safer pursuits.

Eventually Bethany and our chapel were almost finished. A Service of Thanksgiving was arranged for 1st October 1994. God is faithful. When the day arrived the work was done and all the bills paid. The completion and the anticipation of living there made the Thanksgiving a joyful occasion. Lynda composed what we now call her Bethany Song. It resonates with the songs of Miriam and Deborah in the Old Testament. The melody flows in joyful anticipation of the verses still to come.

Come to Your Bethany, Lord Jesus,
We await You with hearts aflame.
Come to be loved, to be cherished,
Come at the call of Your Name.
Come to Your Bethany, Lord Jesus,
Our Bridegroom, our sole darling.
Come to be fed, to be comforted,
Come to Your happy dwelling.

Here is a banquet in Your honour
A feast for a lowly king.
Here are gifts without measure,
Our treasures to You we now bring.
Here is rest and refreshment,
A place to lay down Your head.
Here is love's consolation,
Where love's own yearning is fed.

Here are companions and welcome,
Here there is oil for Your wounds,
Balm for Your sadness and sorrows,
A home where Your happiness abounds.
We greet You, Jesus, with flowers,
Posies of melody and song,
We sprinkle You with love's perfume,
The fragrance of lives laid down.

Here are the friends of Your bosom,
Lovers of Your humble way.
The path of hiddenness and lowliness,
We choose it and prize it through grace.
We bless You now with love's tenderness,
The Brides of Your passion and crown.
We give You our adoration.
Through love's ardent flame we are one.

I Am Yours, Dear Lord, Wherever

"Each Sister has her special place chosen by God and precious in his sight."

"Prayer is not divorced from work: our work is our prayer and an expression of our love for Jesus."

If ever anyone was tested it was Lynda when she was asked to take charge of the work in the kitchen. The Sister who had been doing this was seriously overloaded, as she had responsibilities in other areas as well as cooking. There was little choice but to ask Lynda to take over. We can still see her horrified face. The inevitable "I can't" was her response. Our discipleship, however, is worked out in real life. It took some time, but the grace of the Lord and her giftedness enabled her to excel in this area that included catering and menus, as well as cooking.

It was a big step for Lynda. It was the first time that she was being encouraged to take responsibility on her own, rather than assisting. The Sister whose responsibility it had been deliberately stepped back, so as not to interfere with her decisions. She expresses it well herself in a short Bible study she gave one morning in our chapel:

> I do not know where I would be without wise guidance down the years. On the other hand, this must not result in over-dependence, and an unwillingness to assume responsibility in the various areas of life. Although we will always be grateful for direction at different stages of our Christian journey, there does come a point when we become "God's weaned children".[1] We ourselves are as dearly loved and as cherished as ever, but we are now content to be unnoticed, content to live for others, and to

assume responsibility in whatever area it may be. The lessons of a weaned child are not easy to learn.

The Sister abdicating her position knew that Lynda would learn more from her mistakes and the freedom to make them than from someone being over-protective. All of life is a preparation for heaven. Undoubtedly for Lynda the work in the kitchen was a large part of that preparation. When we are taken out of our comfort zone we become more dependent on the Lord. We learn to trust or go under and Lynda did not go under although she imagined every day for months that she would.

During a retreat with the Evangelical Sisterhood of Mary on Canaan in Germany she notes in her diary, "A joy to see Sister Jochabed – my angel when I was a Canaan helper." On hearing news of Lynda's "promotion" to her new responsibility Sister Jochabed welcomed her by saying, "Here comes our little Brother Lawrence!" Lynda told us about this comment with a broad smile on her face. "The time of business," he had said, "does not with me differ from the time of prayer; and in the noise and clatter of my kitchen, while several persons are at the same time calling for different things, I possess God in as great tranquillity as if I were upon my knees at the Blessed Sacrament." "God lays no great burden upon us, a little remembrance of him from time to time; a little adoration; sometimes to pray for His grace, sometimes to offer him your sorrows, and sometimes to return him thanks for the benefits he has given you, and still gives you in the midst of your troubles."[2] Lynda wasn't quite there but that was her aim:

I have nowhere near reached the heights of Brother Lawrence but often while working in the kitchen I look up to Jesus and say inwardly, "I am yours dear Lord." At the nudging of the Holy Spirit I practise the presence of God in the kitchen. When I am scrubbing potatoes, for instance – with the scrubbing of each potato I express inwardly such words as, "I am loved by the Son, I am loved by the Holy Spirit" – it all depends on how many potatoes there are!

Each morning in the kitchen she tried to give herself anew to the Lord Jesus out of love for him. She fervently asked for the help of the Holy Spirit. Work can become an idol when we love what we are doing and are gifted in it. It is different when it is hard and difficult; something that we would rather not be doing. But it was in the kitchen that the Lord called Lynda to blossom and grow as his bride. She made a note of two more helpful words:

> If contemplation and mental and vocal prayer and the care of the sick and serving about the house and doing menial work, even of the lowest sort, all serve the guest who comes to be with us and to dine and refresh himself with us, why should we concern ourselves whether we serve him in one way or another?
> The Lord is among the saucepans.[3]

Our menus are worked out in advance but rarely work out as planned. Food is sometimes unexpectedly given to us and requires using immediately. We endeavour to use any leftovers. Waste is not encouraged – hence the "soup of the day"! To cook in the community you need to be creative and have the confidence to try new dishes. One day Lynda was given a large quantity of beetroot. She sought advice from her predecessor in the kitchen and together they searched the recipe books for a main course that was primarily beetroot. They found one, a recipe from Russia! One of our visitors takes up the story:

> Sister Lynda informed us that we would be having a special recipe for dinner that she had never cooked before and she looked a little nervous, as the trolley with the food on it came around the corner into the dining room. We all sat in amazement as (vivid) purple food was brought in. Sister

Lynda began placing the food on plates and handing a plate to each guest. Silence filled the room as we contemplated eating it. She explained that it was a Russian recipe, beetroot and potato. We looked around the table at each other then returned our gaze to the plates in silence.

Boldly, one by one we placed a forkful into our mouths, as Sister Lynda watched us tentatively. Amazingly we all really enjoyed it, so much so that we all had second helpings. The tension turned to laughter as we began to chatter and express our surprise. Sister Lynda's smile broadened, as she beamed from ear to ear and there was a glimmer of relief as she murmured, "Thank you, Father."

For a number of years we had a surfeit of gooseberries. The answer was to make them into jam. Unfortunately, gooseberry jam is not everyone's favourite. When Lynda was relatively new to the kitchen, a visitor arrived whose pet hate was gooseberry jam. He hid it, much to Lynda's consternation. She couldn't understand where it had gone, although she suspected the culprit, being well aware of his dislike for that particular jam. Three days later he confessed. It was hidden in the cornflakes. Her sense of humour, never far away in any situation, could not be contained, thankfully for the guilty party, and they laughed together. Life was not without its difficulties!

There was a succession of helpers from several different countries, primarily Switzerland but also Germany, the Czech Republic and Poland. Sometimes she would drive to the airport to meet them and welcome them. Her language skills were very useful. Often they were assisting her in the kitchen. She became a little mother, advisor, teacher and friend, all rolled into one, especially with the younger ones.

Occasionally she had someone helping her who had a difficult personality. She set up a worship corner in the kitchen and began the day's work praying with her helpers. There were "many laughs" as the morning's work progressed. Lynda learnt not only cooking but how to delegate wisely, to be gentle with those who were learning and firm with any who were misbehaving. Her clear-sightedness was a great asset. She was not easily manipulated by anyone, immediately seeing through what was happening and taking a firm line. The strength beneath the gentle exterior that we had glimpsed on other occasions surfaced again when she was in charge of the catering. Our visitors also glimpsed the firmness. One wrote to us, "She brought us to order over lunch one day, when we visitors were chattering too much. We had to be quiet whilst Sister Lynda read to us."

She became an excellent cook. Here too discipline and determination began to show – out went the dumplings beloved by her predecessor. It was the end of the sausage rolls. While she was cooking we were going to eat healthy food! We did! Out went the rice pudding, much to the chagrin of those who loved it. This was for less worthy reasons: she disliked rice pudding. Her mother, a very good cook, came to Lynda's rescue advising, baking and helping on special occasions when we had large buffets. We all loved the simnel cakes at Easter and her delicious Christmas cakes. She baked scones and mince pies. She also helped with beautiful flower arrangements.

When we moved into Redacre the kitchen was antiquated. We improved it but, as the years went by, we were aware that it was woefully small for the amount of activity in it. As someone remarked, if there was more than one person working in the kitchen, it was, "one way around the table". Our domestic gas cooker was too small. We did not have separate sinks for vegetable preparation. We doubted that it would meet the standards of environmental health. The only way to enlarge the kitchen was to extend it outwards and there was a drop of about one and a half metres. Apart from the building work, much of the equipment would need to be upgraded, which would mean more sinks, a commercial cooker, a large stainless steel table and a dishwasher. The electric kettle we used was too small for our needs and a waste of electricity. An efficient water boiler was needed. In effect it would be a new kitchen brought up to an excellent standard. Once again there was a question of finance. Add everything together, the building work and the equipment, and it came to a considerable sum.

We hesitated, but going into the office one day a Sister saw a rather scrappy piece of paper on the desk. We did not recognise the writing and we have never discovered who wrote it but on it were the words, "My God will supply your needs, according to his riches in Christ Jesus."[4] It was the word we needed. It was Lynda and her predecessor who had the joy and anxiety of the refurbishment while other Sisters took responsibility for the building work involved. As always we had to pray our way through. There was no large sum in the bank to cover all the costs.

For a considerable time Redacre kitchen could not be used and everyone still had to be fed. Lynda managed this by running backwards and forwards between our two houses. She was well organised and efficient and most of the time it worked well. Because of the limited facilities in Bethany kitchen, occasionally there were problems. The work in Redacre was eventually completed and we praised God. We met together one evening and dedicated our new kitchen. Together we prayed:

Blessed are you, O Lord our God, King of the Universe,
you gave your word and our kitchen was created.

Blessed are you, O Lord our God, King of the Universe,
provider for your children.
When there was insufficient money,
you heard our prayers,
and provided for the building work
and all the new equipment!

Blessed are you, O Lord our God, King of the Universe,
You provided even those things
that we were willing to do without,
the dishwasher, water heater and table.[5]

Latterly the cooking became less but Lynda remained in overall charge of that and all the catering. She was able to delegate. She was meticulous over cleanliness and taught her helpers to be the same. A sink she cleaned was spotless. As standards were raised nationally she was required, along with those who helped her, to take the Level 2 Award in Food Safety in Catering. We were all nervous – would they pass? We thought that the days of exams were behind us. Three Sisters, a Follower of the Lamb Sister and a friend who helped us took the test. Great was the rejoicing and relief when everyone gained the award. The inspection from Environmental Health, which she had feared unnecessarily, happened not long after she died. We were given the highest grade possible. It was Lynda who had laid the foundations and latterly with other Sisters had successfully brought our kitchen to that standard.

Wherever we are, if we love Jesus, it will show. That is why, as Sisters, it is not what we do that is important but what sort of person we are. Lynda was not perfect, the old enemy anxiety still caused sleepless nights, but she loved God and her will was firmly fixed in serving him. "The simplicity of the gospel, gentleness and compassion can be seen in a smile or a passing word."[6] As butchers, greengrocers and deliverymen came and left, her winning smile welcomed them all. Some opened up their hearts to her. As with everything else, she shopped at speed. She knew exactly what she wanted and where it was. Time was not wasted but she always stopped for a chat with those who needed it. She would come home with stories of folk she had met or the Muslim lady at the checkout who had become a friend.

It would be a mistake to think that Lynda spent all her time in the kitchen – far from it. We deliberately try to keep all necessary heavy work in the house, cooking, cleaning, washing and bed-making, to the morning. As the number of Sisters grew it became easier to be flexible as to who did what and when. Lynda's giftedness took her into many areas. She mastered computers and was then able to help with the accounts, becoming assistant treasurer. She notes in her diary,

> I was quite overwhelmed when I opened a letter this morning to find in it a cheque for £2,000!! – enough (with a little over) to cover the unexpected bills of the past few days! – FATHER, you are wonderful!!

She was skilled at calligraphy and we began to turn to her when we needed greeting cards. She attached a card to her computer. On it in bold italic print were the words,

> Jesus answered, "It is written: 'Worship the Lord your God and serve him only.'"[7]

She had decorated the note with red roses – first love for Jesus. She saw her service to her Sisters and guests alike, as serving the Lord.

Making Music for the Lord

"We are thankful when the Lord reveals to us gifts that he has given of which we were completely unaware."

"We are privileged to love others into the Kingdom of God by our lives and our words, remembering, '. . . we have this treasure in jars of clay to show that this all-surpassing power is from God and not from us.'"[1]

It may have been in our Community Prayers that we first noticed Lynda's beautiful singing voice. She was completely unaware that it was exceptional and as soon as we mentioned it, her throat seemed to close up and she assured us that she couldn't sing! This was shortly after she had joined us. After some coaxing and firmness on our part she accepted that she could sing and that the Lord had given her the gift of a beautiful voice. It seemed to effortlessly soar to the heavens. It was clear and strong but had a sweetness that resonated innocence. There was no affectation. When she sang it was as if her spirit was set free from all the anxiety to which she was prone and she was lifted from a temperament that tended to move more easily towards despair than optimism. "Her voice was uniquely pure and beautiful," wrote one of our friends. As her confidence grew she enjoyed singing, both alone and with others. Her guitar was the instrument she loved and she played it with exceptional sensitivity and skill.

Lynda proved to be a talented musician who had a keen ear and could hear immediately if a note was pitched incorrectly. It wasn't only the guitar, she was a gifted pianist and we loved to hear her play, usually classical music. Possibly, it was an association with the competitions and music examinations in her youth that made her reluctant to play the piano more often. Her parents, after she had been a

Sister for some time, bought her a violin. Sometimes she played this in our chapel. It was the classical guitar that remained her favourite instrument.

With such a gifted musician and other Sisters with musical gifts, it is not surprising that music began to play a central role in our community. All of us, at first, were from a Methodist background and it is said that Methodism was born in song. It never occurred to us not to include hymns in our prayers. We began to introduce modern music. Listening to cassettes and later CDs, Lynda discovered songs with beautiful words and melodies that she then sang. We had another Sister who also played the guitar and they sang together. Eventually there was a large repertoire of music. It was varied, sometimes gentle and reflective and other times quick and lively.

Lynda was never happy about the use of a heavy beat. In a talk she gave she comments:

Music conveys a message like no other medium. Some bands drive home their message of alienation, social change and sex with a heavy beat. But since the beginning of time, God has had a higher purpose for music. He has always wanted to use it to communicate truth and to turn our hearts towards him in worship. Throughout the Bible, the importance of music in worship is stressed again and again.

And as a musician, I am challenged to realise afresh my calling from the Father, to lead my brothers and sisters in worship, into his very presence.

We sang through every situation. When it seemed the way was impossible we sang songs of faith; when we were thankful we put our prayers into song; we even repented in song. We sang of our love for Jesus and the Heavenly Father's love for us.

It was an inevitable next step when we started to use music in weekends that we were leading and for special occasions. As those outside the community became aware of our uplifting music the requests began to come in. Sometimes we were asked if Lynda with another Sister, or later it was Sisters, could sing at a wedding. Lynda sang at her brother's wedding. Sometimes they sang at funerals. This was a ministry in itself. The Sisters were able to bring hope and comfort in these services, a little bit of heaven for those who were grieving. A lady who was fit, hale and hearty and remains so, said to Lynda one day, "Could I book you in advance for my funeral!"

After some time she began to compose her own songs, primarily for special community occasions such as the Thanksgiving Service for Bethany, Bridal Consecrations, Christian Festivals, and from time to time a song because it came to her, a gift from the Holy Spirit. Sometimes she wrote her own words and other times, she used words from different sources. Her music mostly had guitar accompaniment. She worked out the chords so that other Sisters could accompany the singing with their instruments. Later a Sister was able to transcribe them.

She composed a haunting lament and sang it as we remembered the suffering of Jesus in Gethsemane on Maundy Thursday. The high notes were piercing in their grief. No one who heard it will ever forget that lament. Her heart and soul were in it, as she sang:

My Father
If it is possible
May this cup be taken from me

My Father
If it is possible
May this cup be taken from me

Yet not as I will
But as You will

My Father
My Father

Yet not as *I* will
But as You will

My Father
My Father

My Father
If it's not possible
For this cup to be taken away

My Father
If it's not possible
For this cup to be taken away

Unless *I* drink it
Unless *I* drink it
Unless *I* drink it
Unless *I* drink it

May Your will be done
May Your will be done
May Your will be done.[2]

She prepared our Easter Vigil for Holy Saturday, composing some of the music and writing the words. Again there was a beautiful song, which she sang herself:

Sabbath rest, O peace most holy,
Sabbath rest, O peace divine;
Jesus lies in the arms of the Father,
All the shouts around Him die.

Come adore Him, come adore Him,
Worship the Lamb that was slain.
Come adore Him, come adore Him;
Worship the Lamb, slain for us.

Now the agony is over,
Now the sacrifice complete;
Jesus hides in the kiss of the Father,
From all pain and grief released.

Let our tears anoint His suffering,
In soft linen silent lies;
Let us now bow down before Him,
Await the day when He shall rise.

In our quiet chapel with a single red rose lying on a white lace cloth beneath the cross, her sweet voice echoed with love for Jesus.

In the song she composed for Easter Day, the alleluias cascade and the joy overflows. We sing this composition regularly in our Sunday Morning Prayers. Lynda's music helped to make Easter memorable for our visitors and us each year.

Alleluia, alleluia, Jesus is risen,
Truly he is risen.
Out of the tomb, forth he came,
with great glory and majesty,
Alleluia, alleluia, alleluia.

Alleluia, alleluia, Jesus is Victor,
Conqueror by the Cross,
He will take us into glory,
all our hope, our joy in Him.
Alleluia, alleluia, alleluia.

Alleluia, alleluia, the Lord of Life died,
but now He lives and reigns.
Oh once again he's close beside us.
Now forever, alleluia.
Alleluia, alleluia, alleluia.

Alleluia, alleluia, glory! Lord of life!
Sinners now reconciled.

And we His lambs skip for joy
On green pastures, ever after.
Alleluia, alleluia, alleluia.[3]

The alleluias tumble out in the last verse. It consists wholly of alleluias – eleven of them.

Evenings of music such as Advent Praise and the Adoration of the Christ Child at Christmas were inspirational and greatly loved by all who experienced them. One of her regrets was that, as her responsibilities grew, she had less time for composing. She needed space and quietness and this was often denied her. She could not compose to order but needed stillness to hear the Holy Spirit. Maybe that is why one of her most beautiful melodies was given to her on Holy Island. As you listen to the music you can almost hear the tide ebbing and flowing around the island that she loved.

The Bible Comes Alive

"The up-front jobs, which are often seen quite wrongly as the most important, are to be approached with humility. Do not seek to be self-important. The Pharisees did that and Jesus said, 'I tell you the truth, they have received their reward in full.'"[1]

Lynda had no difficulty playing her guitar and singing in front of a large number, but Bible studies were a different matter. When the subject was first broached we were back again to the "I can't". The need for another Sister to be available to teach and lead was becoming increasingly obvious. We were leading Bible studies regularly. In addition we began to include a short comment on the verses for the day in our morning prayers. We had become convinced that in some churches there was a dearth of good teaching from Scripture. We knew that she had the ability to teach although there were limits on her time. Often, as she prepared she would be first teaching herself.

She had been with us long enough to appreciate the spiritual dangers of the up-front jobs. There is a subtle temptation to pride. This is aided and abetted by the culture around us. Status is important and this often goes with the work a person does. Some tasks are judged to be more menial than others. God looks at the heart, not our status in the eyes of the world. It takes a long time to learn this lesson. Lynda shared in a Bible study:

> In my earlier days of responsibility in the kitchen, when I did not want to work in such a place of the "Father's choosing", because I felt it was beneath me, I stuck a prayer on one of the walls: "O Jesus, King of humility, you shall not go the way of lowliness alone. I want to

accompany you."[2] Today we can tell him anew that we want to throw away our pride, our desire for attention or to be popular and that we want to walk the humble way, close by his side.

That is why it is important for every Sister to do work with her hands; what the world sees as menial work. Lynda had found freedom working in the kitchen because her freedom was in Christ. Status ceased to matter and her sense of worth came from the certainty that she was a child of the Heavenly Father. She saw clearly that there was no place for intellectual pride, or pride in one's own gifts. She comments:

> We will not be judged according to the knowledge we have amassed, even Biblical knowledge; we will not be judged and welcomed by the apparent success of our ministries or due to a special giftedness in a certain direction. Jesus will only be concerned with whether we have loved or not, and that in a practical way.

She didn't take too seriously remarks such as, "We loved your talk this morning." She was free to illustrate from her own failures in order to help others. There was no superiority, no putting herself on a pedestal, as one who had all the answers. When she spoke, it was refreshing in its lack of preachiness. Well-grounded in the grace of God, she managed to steer clear of the heavy "oughts", "musts" and "shoulds". Rather like her singing, there was a refreshing simplicity in her style. Her imagination, which often worked to her disadvantage when she was anxious, became an asset when she was teaching from the Bible. She could vividly see characters and scenes from the Bible in her mind and was able to bring them to life.

Lynda's sense of humour could at times be outrageous. Even when the response should have been disapproval it was difficult to suppress a smile. When disapproval came she was undismayed and carried on regardless. Added to this she could impersonate, which made her recounting of incidents extremely funny. She often made us laugh. Her sense of humour was reflected in the Bible studies she gave. She delighted in informing us that the Egyptian Pharaoh, the mighty Ramases II, with his eyeliner, was an "Egyptian makeover of Elizabeth Taylor". It is not difficult either to see Jacob from Lynda's description, "hanging around the encampment and lurking around the tents". His twin, Esau, she described as "feckless and reckless". The Pharisees and Teachers of the Law waiting for Jesus were "in a flurry of ruffled feathers".

Amos addressed the wealthy women of Samaria as "the cows of Bashan".[3] This appealed to her sense of humour, although it is doubtful whether Amos intended it to be humorous. Lynda commented with approval, "Amos doesn't mince his words!" She wasn't slow to draw a parallel with the affluence of some in the 21st century. Her Bible studies were never boring. She was able to use a light touch to lead into serious teaching.

She had the misfortune to be on our rota for the talk in our morning prayers when we had three bishops joining us. We had not had much contact with bishops. Not unnaturally Lynda was worried about it. The passage was Romans 8:1–8. With a nervous swallow and speaking quickly, she began:

This is one of the best known, best loved chapters of the whole Bible. When I was twenty years old and in a pit of depression, Sister Eulalia – a German Sister – said, "Memorise Romans 8 – ze whole of it – Vunderful medicine for ze soul!"

Her impression of a Sister from Darmstadt speaking English with a German accent was quite memorable. Then she added:

I have never forgotten her advice – but I have forgotten some of the verses!

Even the sternest-looking bishop was having difficulty keeping his face straight. Once her nervousness subsided, she gave a very good talk.

She was quick to illustrate from her own experience, knowing that in this way she could build a bridge to her listeners and then lead them through to the truth in Christ. Some would see it as making herself vulnerable but she had long since passed the place where she tried to be anything other than what she actually was. Her security was in Christ. There was no question in her mind about vulnerability. On one occasion she shared:

How often do we dwell under a cloud of condemnation – "I have blown it this time" – I was so unthinking or unloving in that situation – I can't really be forgiven this time, or that mistake I made was too big this time! We come to Jesus in repentance but still feel condemned – this is because our pride gets in the way. Jesus has borne our condemnation, there is none left for us in Christ Jesus! And I speak to myself first and foremost.

This was the old battleground for Lynda as it is for many people. Now she saw it and the way through. She was throwing out a lifeline from her own experience to others caught in the same place. In all her Bible studies she showed her own self-awareness. Sometimes she deliberately shared but other times her self-knowledge quite unconsciously slips out:

Some fifteen years ago, I remember Jean Darnell's words to me as I approached her for prayer at the end of a meeting, my smile betraying nothing.

Many times Lynda's lovely smile was masking anxiety, as Jean clearly saw when she prayed over her. Lynda spoke about this in the context of a Bible study from Matthew

6:25–34. She heads it, "Is worry a sin? It is." She shares more of her own difficulties in this area with a certain wry humour and without condemnation, before she points to the way through:

> We read, with regard to the lilies, that, "they do not labour or spin". "Spin" probably means here "to weave", but another kind of spinning came into my mind, one that I am particularly good at! Our quick, impatient movements often betray our inner worry/anxiety, or if we are unable to move quickly, then our worry is betrayed by an abruptness and impatient words. We spin around in a panic when we have a lot to fit in. I am known to some of my Sisters as "Flash Lynda"! People usually fail to see me; instead they see the cloud of dust that I leave in my tracks. The other day, for instance, as we discussed the flowers which were in a vase in the hall, a Sister pointed out, not without a little rebuke, "If you had passed the flowers at a slightly more leisurely pace, then you would have noticed that most of them had died!" The Lord Jesus has spoken to me on numerous occasions about the need to "tread softly in the fold",[4] i.e. to go carefully and calmly about my business.

She speaks of "anxiety exhausting our inner resources". This had been her experience. She points to trust as the way through. "The Father waits for us to tread his path, the path of childlike trust in him." In the years following this Bible study she continued to grow in the grace and love of God that casts out all fear. It was, however, always a difficult area for her.

Scenes from the Bible were described in such a way that you felt you were there! She was certainly there herself. One of her favourite phrases was, "We can imagine the scene."

> When Peter left Jerusalem for Galilee, where else would he go but home? And when it came to a night's fishing surely he would take his own family boat, drawn up on a section

of the beach the family always used – the place where they draped their nets over the rough grey rocks to dry, where they sorted and sold fish. We imagine the disciples clambering into the boat. We listen to the water, the small waves lapping against its wooden hull. In the night's silence we hear the boat creak with every movement and the shuffle of feet as the companions stretch and change position. We feel the boat rock as they move. The thwarts (the seats) they sit on are hard, unyielding. There's limited space for seven men with nets and baskets, the sails and oars, and all the other equipment they need. The disciples sit quietly. There's just an occasional gruff direction from Peter, in charge of the family boat. Conversation is quickly exhausted. Hour after hour passes. The chill night damp enfolds them. Again and again the nets are hauled up and let down, but in vain; not a single fish enters them.

In this Bible study she continues:

This night of empty nets and possibly empty spirits is a gift from God to the disciples, though they will only see it in retrospect. For ourselves too, the night, figuratively speaking, when all seems without purpose and clarity, is a gift, for at such times we come to realise who we are and who God is. We come to realise that it is his love which is arranging all, in order to teach us the deepest lessons that ever entered our hearts, usually lessons connected with humility. There is not a cross, a loss, a disappointment, a case of failure in our lives, which is not arranged and controlled by our loving Lord Jesus, and intended to teach us lessons which we could learn in no other way.

Her visit to Israel enabled her descriptions of scenes in the Bible to become even more vivid:

This pebble here is very precious (show pebble). No, it did not come from around one of our ponds in the garden, or even from West Kirby beach, but from the very spot I have just been talking about – "Simon Peter's Landing Place" on the shore of Lake Galilee, or Tiberias or Kinneret. And here is a photograph of the Franciscan church near this special place. I can still hardly believe it but I was standing on this very shore only last month. It was such a privilege.

The rocky shore surrounding Lake Galilee is probably much the same as it was when Jesus walked there – unspoilt. The same landscape greets our eyes; the lapping of the waves sounds as it did of old. As I stood by the water's edge, a sense of timelessness embraced me and I almost expected to see Jesus, from the corner of my eye, walking towards me! It is that unspoilt! We also had the privilege of viewing this spot from a distance, from the Mount of Beatitudes and also from a boat (similar to that which Jesus and his disciples would have used) in the middle of Galilee. That was an indescribable experience!

The following year the wonder of that visit is still there. On Maundy Thursday she shares her feelings when she saw the ancient olive trees in the garden of Gethsemane and later knelt before the Rock of Christ's Agony in the Church of All Nations:

My Spirit knew beyond doubt that this is where Jesus suffered for me.

Her good memory enabled her to quote from books that she had read. She loved the writings of the Saints and their lives. For instance, "He became what we were that we might become what he is! Alleluia."[5] "God loves each one of us as if there was only one of us."[6] "He (God) wraps and enfolds us, embraces and encloses us, in Love."[7] Many such memorable quotes were included in her talks. In one talk alone she quotes from Thomas à Kempis, Janet Erskine Stuart, St Gregory and St Francis de Sales. The latter was probably her favourite. "My friend, Francis de Sales," she wrote. He was the wise and gentle Bishop of Geneva. "Consider the eternal love, which God has borne towards you; for our Lord Jesus Christ, as man, suffered on the cross for you, His Divine Majesty contemplated you in his Sovereign goodness and loved you exceedingly."[8]

In a study on Jacob, she spoke about the "wonderful transformation" after his encounter with God at the Jabbock Brook. "God dearly loves those who are broken: he can't bear to part with them," she commented. Lynda once heard a Brother from another community say, "When the sun is away (i.e. the leader of the community) then the moon can shine." This happened with Lynda. When those who were leading the community were away, "the moon shone". We became aware that unsuspected qualities of leadership were there. It is not surprising that we all began to see in her the future leader of the community or, as we say, the role of "Little Sister". If we mentioned this to her the "I can't" sprang into action. As all the evidence pointed in the other direction we were confident that one day she would fulfil that role.

Inwardly she gave the Father her "yes". On 11th September 2007 she wrote in her diary,

While I was sitting on the hill gazing out towards the estuary I asked the Father to give me a word of Scripture within the next few days, concerning the community's future and my part – immediately Joshua 1:9 sprang into my mind and I knew that the Holy Spirit had spoken. I am so blessed! I read the whole chapter when I returned to my room – very apt! When I opened Joshua 1 my eyes immediately fell upon the words, "Be strong and courageous because you will lead these people." – And v.9 reads, "Be strong and courageous. Do not be terrified, do not be discouraged, for the Lord your God will be with you wherever you go." My Father, I am willing, if you lead me. I am fearful and weak but I look to your promise.

When she was a young Sister she wrote down some advice given to her by Sister Divina:

Always have a "yes" for your Sisters, even in the busiest of days, always have a "yes", so that your Sisters can feel in their hearts that they can go to Lynda because there is a warmth in her heart for them, and a willingness to help, wherever possible. Often no words are needed, only a warm smile.

It was good advice to a young Sister but it was also prophetic, because that was what happened, and there are Sisters within the community who have cause to be grateful.

All God's Creatures

"We delight in and give thanks for the God-given things."

Simplicity is a promise that we make but on our journey it also becomes a way of life that we embrace. We begin to look at the world around us in a new and different way. The best things in life are free and greet us every day if only we have eyes to see them. There is an innocence and wonder in childhood that is lost as we become adult. Part of our journey with God is a restoration of that lost innocence. Lynda delighted in much that others passed by without a backward glance. She describes crossing Westminster Bridge: "On viewing the Houses of Parliament, Big Ben and the Thames embankment all lit up in the twilight, something in me wanted to exclaim, 'Wow!'"

Life itself was vividly alive for her. She was not an emotional person but she felt deeply. Even her body reflected the same sensitivity; slight asthma caused us to be cautious with perfumes when she was around. Anxiety could produce skin troubles. Her vivid imagination was both a gift and a problem. Her sensitivity extended to her hearing, which was acute. She heard sounds most of us missed. At times this was helpful; other times it was difficult for other Sisters who forgot and cheerfully closed a door a bit too enthusiastically. It was the same sensitivity that made her acutely aware of pain and the beauty of music. It contributed to her gentle nature but it meant she could easily interpret correction as rejection. She knew the heights of joy but could plummet to the depths of despair. She was like a finely tuned instrument.

Simplicity of life and her sensitive nature came together when she looked in childlike wonder at the beautiful world around her. A friend in Monmouth described a time when Lynda stayed with her for a few days: "I took her to see an eagle fly. She loved it and I remember on that day being moved by her joy and delight."

She loved the ever-changing Dee Estuary. A beautiful dawn or sunset brought equal enjoyment. Rainbows spoke to her –

A rainbow on the beach in the midst of high winds and hail – God is with us in the storms of life.

I see rainbows everywhere, another one today whilst in West Kirby. They seem to accompany me and are a sign that God is with me.

She delighted in the wildlife in our garden. We dug ponds and great was our delight one spring morning when the mallards flew in. Frogs arrived in droves at spawning time. At dusk on warm summer evenings Lynda could be seen watching the bats in swift flight over the water. Although we had mixed feelings about the heron and our pond was soon barricaded like a fort, we still admired this beautiful bird. He strutted over our lawn with a proprietary air, quite at home.

One Sunday, as we were eating our lunch, the doorbell rang. We were in Bethany and answered via the intercom. A lady informed us that there was a duck in our front drive with ten ducklings. Lynda, with other Sisters, raced to the front drive. It was a mallard. We opened the garden gate and the little procession came down the path, negotiated the waterfall and landed in our pond. Eight admirers crowded around the pond and from that moment they became "our chicks". They were delightful; little balls of fluff from which protruded a tiny head and two spindly legs.

It was a sunny day and they scrambled out of the water onto a small rock, snuggling close together and to their mother. Space was at a premium. Ten is rather a large family and the last one out kept sliding down the smooth stone back into the pond! He didn't give up! We saw the care that the female takes with her young. She noticed and moved slightly until there was room for all. Her care for her little ones was touching to watch and reminded us of the watchfulness of God with us. "The Lord watches over you."[1]

After a rest she marched the ten fluffy yellow and brown chicks around the garden, strengthening their little legs and reconnoitering her route for the next day. Night came and she settled by the side of the pond with all ten under her wings, ready to die for them if they were attacked. Not one little head or tail could be seen. Secure under her wings, they rested. It was impossible not to think of Jesus as he wept over Jerusalem. "How often I have longed to gather your children together, as a hen gathers her chicks under her wings, but you were not willing!"[2] There are many verses in Scripture about the shelter of God's wings. "How priceless is your unfailing love! Both high and low among men find refuge in the shadow of your wings."[3] "I will take refuge in the shadow of your wings until the disaster has passed."[4]

The male settled on the path beside them. The ducklings were contented and secure but we were worried as we have foxes passing through our garden. We beseeched the Heavenly Father that night to protect them from harm. Great was our relief the next day on waking to see the ten bundles of fluff energetically swimming in the pond with the female beside them.

Later that morning the mother set off along the Praise Path with the ten chicks close behind her. Unhesitatingly she led them next door through a small gap. Some garden rubbish then enabled them to negotiate the wall and over they went. She chose the place where it is terraced but nevertheless, to a tiny duckling each descent must have seemed like falling over a cliff. They landed, much to the surprise of those who lived beneath us, outside their back door; all, that is, except one unfortunate who landed in the wrong garden. The female knew one was lost. Great was the quacking and chirping until a little form speeded under the hedge to rejoin them. Lynda was there, anxious for the safety of the chicks and delighted with their progress.

Our neighbour opened the garden gate and the little procession passed through, down their front path, across a road and down the street opposite. She walked them across another road and into the park. There was still quite a way to go across the park but the little ones kept up, as she didn't slacken her pace. We have a picture of them a few yards from the lake, the mother with her neck stretched towards the water anticipating with eagerness the journey's end, and the little ones close behind her, all ten safely home. Perseverance is a great quality.

Almost every day one of us went down to see them; all ten chicks survived. The fluffy down gave way to feathers as they matured. We didn't witness their first flight, but next spring, when the mallards flew high overhead or skidded to a halt as they splashed down in our ponds, we wondered if it was one of our chicks come back.

Lynda observed with a keen eye the wildlife in our garden. This became increasingly necessary as squirrels stole our bulbs, woodpigeons our soft fruit and blackbirds in a dawn raid devoured all our cherries, leaving the stones on the path! She wrote:

We enjoyed some light entertainment by a cheeky squirrel just beyond the raspberry bushes. He grabbed the head of a sunflower, proceeded to take its petals off one by one before devouring the seeds in the middle. This little comedy was then repeated before he flung himself onwards towards the raspberry bushes and began to pick some raspberries in a very 'human-like' way. That was quite enough, I flew out of the back door violently clapping my hands only to find myself being watched by a couple of guests from the bedroom windows. God's creatures (including myself) can be extremely funny at times.

The colourful jays drew equal delight with the woodpecker working its way up the trunk of one of our beech trees. When it was night the ghostly call of the owl resounded in the darkness. In the garden Lynda found solace and closeness to God. She and the Sister who accompanied her to Clatterbridge Centre for Oncology had become close friends with Kevin, a patient they had met there. They had the joy of hearing his first prayer and our vicar, the joy of giving him his first communion. Kevin died and Lynda described the day of his funeral and the consolation she later found in the solitude of our garden.

It was Kevin's funeral today and a day of glorious sunshine. The church was full – mostly clad in black – we stood out like a summer's day in our heavenly blue. There were harrowing scenes – he was greatly loved. After returning home I took a walk around our peaceful garden. A wonderful gift from the Heavenly Father awaited me – there high up on the branch of a beech tree, stood a song thrush perched against a bright blue sky, singing its little heart out – and what beautiful melodies it sang – they filled our garden. In these moments I knew deep in my heart that there is a Heaven containing even more beauty than this scene did – and that Kevin was surely there.

She later wrote:

We live in a beautiful world!
Miniature irises in the pots by our doorway
An amaryllis bursting forth triumphantly in our dining
     room
Ten geese in flight in the twilight
A calm mill-pond-ish estuary.
Father, your stamp is everywhere if we have but eyes to
     see.

She had the eyes to see. Often she was the first, after the Sister who tended the flowerbeds, to see new blooms bursting into life as the seasons came and went.

God's creatures were even nearer to home than the wildlife in the garden. For many years we have had a cat and a dog. They have been greatly loved, not least by Lynda. Her strongest affection was for the dog. We acquired a labrador cross, Timothy, that a dog warden had brought in. He was about ten months old, only a puppy. The vet described him as a street urchin on our first visit, which wasn't surprising, as he had created near mayhem in the waiting area. He also said that he had the makings of a good dog, and so he became. Ill-treatment during those early months had left scars that always made us feel extra-protective towards him. He in turn was protective towards us. One day when Lynda was walking him on the lead some youths became threatening. Timothy advanced towards them, growling, and they fled.

He was with us for 14 years enjoying life with great abandon. One April morning, the Praise Path a carpet of bluebells and the grass softened by gentle rain, we watched, as our vet brought Timmy's life to a gentle end. Along with the rest of us, Lynda was heartbroken:

Timothy, our beloved and gentle dog was put to sleep on our lawn this morning (9.15 a.m.).

He was a special dog, who died gently too. We shall miss him dreadfully. I shall miss my playmate. I can't believe he's gone . . . where has he gone?

But Lord Jesus, your kindness was everywhere today – in the vet, in the timing (guests at breakfast), that he could die on our lawn – he loved to be out of doors.

That evening after night prayer we glanced out of the chapel window and to our astonishment, as we had already had one brood earlier in the year, there were little chicks on the edge of our chapel pond with the female mallard hovering nearby. Dusk began to fall and she tucked them safely under her wings. It was a picture of the Father's love for us.

After two months without a dog we began to pray for one. We contacted a nearby animal rescue organisation and were informed that there was a 2-year-old collie/retriever cross, Thomas, needing a new home. He was good with people. This turned out to be an understatement! There was a problem – the cat. The re-homer promised to find out if Thomas was good with cats. When we heard nothing, we presumed that he had failed the cat test. After a further phone call, when it looked as if it was going to take some time to find the right dog, we were feeling rather discouraged. Five minutes later the phone rang and it was the re-homer from the animal rescue. Thomas had no experience of cats. We contacted his owner. He was a much-loved dog but her circumstances had changed. To cut a long story short, after a few visits Thomas moved in. Our hearts went out to the young woman and to the bewildered dog as they parted company. We loved Fran, almost as much as we loved Thomas. She comes to visit, and pictures are often sent to her.

The cat was a problem! To be more accurate, the cat and the dog together were a problem! At first they were both afraid of each other. Then they gathered confidence, which meant the cat slid out from behind a chair, tapped the bemused dog on the nose and retreated fast. Thomas discovered the joys of chasing. Then, true to his loving nature, as the cat lay sleepily in her basket in the morning Thomas tenderly washed her all over with his tongue. Unfortunately, the cat didn't always appreciate his ministrations, especially as they became more enthusiastic each passing morning. This tender show of affection didn't stop him chasing her during the remainder of the day. In the animal kingdom, as well as the human kingdom, relationships can be hard work! They need perseverance, much prayer and trust in the Heavenly Father! They are now best friends, most of the time!

Lynda loved Thomas. She had found a new playmate.

Holy Island Diary

"Times of recreation should be used wisely in order to restore body, mind and spirit. There is a balance between being together and solitude."

We spend many of our breaks on Lindisfarne, or Holy Island as it is more frequently called. Lynda kept a journal of her first visit there in the middle of winter 2001. She fell in love with this beautiful island in Northumberland, a love that she never lost. She kept a diary while she was there. Again and again she expresses a childlike wonder. She wrote:

"Thursday, 8th February

I arrived here on Holy Island, just before the lunch-time tide was about to engulf the causeway. I was greeted with glorious skies and sunshine. As we approached this 'place of peace', I felt like a princess riding the Royal Mile – I sensed, somehow, the honouring of my King.

Felt (and feel) very weary, very low in my spirit, but the gentle love of God has already begun to steal into my 'battle worn' soul . . . I was especially aware of his gentleness while gazing at St Cuthbert's Island against the fiery sunset sky – and again as I stroked the velvety nose of the horse, whose home is opposite St Mary's Church where evening prayer is held. His (God's) gentleness also whispered that I am not to be afraid, that he knows all things.

We attended evening prayer (5.30 p.m.) – aware immediately of the eternal-ness of God whilst kneeling in the chancel of this lovely old church. The rhythm of his eternal faithfulness found its echo in the rhythmic reading of the Psalms. The verse came into my mind, 'From everlasting to everlasting you are God.'[1] Feel safe here within this church –

upon this Island simply to 'be'. My Friend will disclose Himself to me. It will be a gentle disclosure.

God's power finds a pale reflection in the power of the sea. High tide today. Gulls – hundreds of them – rioting on the crest of the waves – a spectacular sight!

Friday, 9th February

My quiet room/bedroom (!) boasts a superb and direct view of Lindisfarne Castle, which looked incredibly beautiful – and strong – clothed in the light of the sunrise this morning.

Mid-morning we set off to St Cuthbert's Island (safe to cross there two hours or so after first safe crossing time) – Cuthbert spent time in prayer on this Isle, but the people 'pressed in upon' him even there, so eventually he made Inner Farne his sanctuary, where he was left mostly in peace to be with his God – the rough waters between rendered him virtually inaccessible. Bliss – I imagine!!

I like St Cuthbert's Island – the remains of his little cell, the stark wooden cross at its heart, gently dominating the skyline. The seaweed is unusual in appearance – vast amounts of it – very slippery!

We returned via the Priory ruins. We stopped for a short while outside the Priory walls, and 'listened' to the peace of God. After lunch we set off towards the harbour – sat on a hilly bit overlooking the sea, the mainland and Bamburgh Castle. The waters were very still and milky – everything bathed in tranquil sunlight – so profoundly peaceful. God's whispers were carried to me by the gentle lapping of the waves – 'my dear daughter, let me cradle you in my peace.'

Gentleness yesterday. Peace today. No need to fear. Fascinating watching the fishing boats coming in surrounded by hungry gulls, hopeful for something from the catch. Watched rugged-faced fishermen dragging in crates of crab – still alive. Apparently it hadn't been a particularly successful catch. A hard morning's work for such a small catch. Jesus knows what they feel like – he is still waiting for them on the shore.

David Adam writes in his life of St Aidan – 'Just as life is a battle, it is also a journey, a pilgrimage, a moving on. One of the great curses of life is to become stuck, and unable to move. Once movement stops we begin to die. The Irish monk and missionary, Columbanus said that, "Life is not a resting place – life is a road!" Let us ever ponder on the end of the road, that is, of life, for the end of the roadway is our home.'[2]

Happy this evening because I've just been informed that I will be able to spend the week alone here after all! Jesus knows the desire of our hearts!

At the beginning of evening prayer David Adam, Vicar of Holy Island, quoted some words of Jesus quite unexpectedly and seemingly unconnected with the rest of this evening's liturgy, but I was deeply moved. All I can say is that the Holy Spirit underlined these words for me.

Jesus said, 'You did not choose me, but I chose you.'[3]

Jesus seems to want to impress this truth more deeply into my wavering heart, the importance of and the security issuing from being chosen by Him.

Sunday, 11th February

After lunch we set out on a relatively long hike across the links towards Emmanuel Head. Nearly swept off our feet by the strong winds as we arrived at our destination, marked by a huge white stone pyramid. It was wonderful to be able to sit together and watch the powerful sea. The ocean is so vast and relentless. We talked about the old Celtic saints who wrote, understandably, strong prayers to the Three in One. They needed to address the Holy Trinity in such a way – 'Holy Strong One' – in the face of the powerful elements and the 'Powerful One'.

Our joy was made complete when I spotted a seal's head bobbing up and down in the rough waters. Perseverance was the name of the game!! These creatures are quite incredible and have much to teach us!

We went to see the Causeway at high tide on this 'strong winds' day. What a marvellous sight! For the first time I really felt – as though – and saw, that I was truly on an island, absolutely cut off from the mainland.

Monday, 12th February

This morning, set off towards the harbour, in the direction of the Castle. Settled myself down against a rock and began my meditations on the Gospel of John. 'And from his fullness have we all received, grace upon grace'[4] stayed with me. Later walked onto the Heugh and sat facing the sea, in the warmth of the sunlight. I reflected on the fullness of Jesus – much, much fuller than the fullness and vastness of the North Sea. I have been a deeply blessed recipient of His grace. I feel it is an enormous privilege to be here.

Wednesday, 14th February

Smiled as I passed the Castle, a grey pigeon eyed me suspiciously from one of the turrets! A 'malnourished' thane from the 7th century, jealously guarding Lindisfarne!!

This afternoon we walked to the shore beyond the Castle where there are particularly beautiful views of the Farne Isles. An idyllic, heavenly day. No words to describe it. How beautiful heaven must be!

Thursday, 15th February

Delighted to see a pair of goldfinches as I opened the back door earlier. Beautiful little birds . . . their heads are so red! First evening alone. My 'iris' cross-stitch has become an 'intercession' cross-stitch; it is a good way of praying for dear ones without becoming too intense about it.

Friday, 16th February

After doing some washing, left house just after 9.30 a.m. – the sunlight was beckoning me! My first friend to greet me near the Heugh (near the harbour) was a song thrush, needless to say, singing its little heart out – settled myself down on one of the benches, which looks towards the mainland. Began to read Daily Light, the first two verses drew my attention – read no further: 'Christ loved us and gave himself up for us as a fragrant offering and sacrifice to God.'5 'Now to you who believe, this stone is precious.'6

Immediately – gazing at the gently lapping waters, the sunlight, the Cheviots in the distance – I knew that the Lord Jesus was saying to me something like, 'You need no other love but mine. My love for you is all-sufficient. It reaches the deepest places of your being if you will allow it to.'

St Cuthbert's Island: I prayed that I could be alone here for a little while, and I was! I stood facing the big cross for some minutes – strong and high. Then gathered a piece of rock and cast it into the sea . . . saw the piece of rock as representing my sin of unbelief – which now is cast into the ocean of his redeeming love. Jesus' blood cleanses me from this, and every sin. I picked up another piece of rock, which I saw as symbolising my 'self-love' – that too I hurled into the waters beneath me.

Jesus stood by my side. He has witnessed and he has sealed. I settled down on a large rock, leaning back on some rock behind me, and basked in the sun. It has been so warm today, just like a summer's day with barely a cloud in the sky – what a gift!

I watched 18 eider ducks, affectionately known as cuddy ducks (Cuthbert's beloved friends), to-ing and fro-ing in front of me on the waters – definitely the mating season. One drake did his display act to woo a female – pressed his bill down to touch his breast, then he jerked his head upright and called to the female something like, 'coo-roo-ah'. Other drakes followed suit, what a funny sight! I almost laughed aloud – never seen anything like it before.

Whilst still sitting on the rock read a little from 'The Normal Christian Life'.7 I have asked Jesus (and the Spirit) to open the eyes of my heart so that I might know that I have been crucified with Christ, died with him and have been buried with him . . . I read earlier in John's Gospel that, 'Man can receive only that which is given him from heaven.'8 Only Jesus can give the necessary revelation from heaven, and on

Wednesday he promised me, as he did Nathanael, that I will 'see the heavens opened'.[9] I abandon myself to him.

Saturday, 17th February

Made my way slowly to the Heugh again this morning – another very beautiful day with a gentle breeze – the sun creating a pathway of diamonds across the waters, towards where I was sitting, this time on the rocks at the water's edge. I had some eider ducks as companions some distance away.

Enjoying John's Gospel still – imagined Jesus sitting beside me on the rocks, just as he sat with the Samaritan woman at the well. Told him how glad I am that he knows everything about me. As with Nathanael, Jesus' knowledge of the woman's life opened her eyes to who he was . . . and the truth set her free! What a wonderful moment when she spoke the words, 'I know that Christ is coming. When he comes, he will explain everything to us.' Then Jesus declared, 'I who speak to you am he.'[10] Sang, 'Open my eyes Lord . . .' at the water's edge.

After lunch, set off 'walking in the name of Jesus Christ' (!) along the Straight Lonnen towards the eastern shore. En route surprised to see two peacocks, one within the farmyard and the other opposite the farmyard entrance. Then to my amusement I came across what looked like a turkey taking a bath in the filthiest puddle, in the middle of the Lonnen. He ignored me totally, obviously totally 'immersed' in his ablutions! I enjoyed the walk in a fresher, cooler air than yesterday. The sun had lost its earlier warmth . . . sat for a while in the direction of the Farne Islands reading Nee's book again, helpful bit today: 'How do we abide?'

Sunday, 18th February

Walked again to the Heugh – it's amazing that despite the number of people on the Island today, I saw no one come near the 'prayer holes' – quite a secluded spot. Read some of Sister Divina's old letters to me. She must have almost despaired of me at times!

Watched eider duck and drake bob up and down together in the fairly rough waters. No more need for the mating call – he had won his 'bride' – a picture of tranquillity and contentment, as they went off together to find a nesting place. 'Maybe that's how it is with you and me, Jesus! You have wooed me and now it is simply a matter of stepping forth contentedly in your companionship. You in love with me, and I in love with you!'

Monday, 19th February

Later in the morning made my way once again to the Heugh – 'My Trysting Place' with Jesus. The sun was so hot there that I had to remove some articles of clothing. It was wonderful to feel the strong warmth of the sun on my face and arms. Recommenced my meditations on the Gospel of John. The fishermen here were just coming into the harbour as I read the part where the 'fishermen of old' saw Jesus approaching their boat, walking on the water, and they were terrified, and Jesus spoke, 'It is I! Don't be afraid.'[11] It struck me again that Jesus was no wimp, meek and mild in the wrong sense. He came first to rugged, usually fearless fishermen. He was a man of men with a powerful Gospel to proclaim. I could almost see Jesus walking on the water between Holy Island and the mainland, approaching the fishing boat! That would have frightened the wits out of these rough, Island fishermen and their seagull friends.

Tuesday, 20th February

Made for 'my spot' again this morning, but winds too cold to sit for long . . . managed a closer look at the eider ducks – the rocks down by the Heugh being their terminus this morning – lovely colouring – plumage. A further distance away I spotted a cormorant or shag (I'm not quite sure which). I love all these different species of birds. I shall miss them. I feel a thrill of wonder each time a flock of oystercatchers or a gaggle of geese fly past.

Wednesday, 21st February

My final day alone! Thank you, Lord Jesus, for this special time of solitude. Thank you for wrapping me around with kindness, with beauty, with your love, with so much more!

Walked to the Heugh again this morning at 10.00 a.m. – spectacular cloud formation – the first time I've seen this wonder on the Island. Oh to be able to capture it on canvas! As I stood surveying the clouds, a gaggle of seemingly hyperactive geese flew by; some of them appeared to be arguing in flight – quite a hostile bunch! Put a smile on my face.

After lunch, set off towards the harbour – this time with binoculars . . . spotted a seal with my naked eye, but by the time I had assembled my binoculars (strange pair) he had disappeared underwater! My friends were there – the eider ducks! A lone fisherman appeared in his boat. I do so love this Island. When I leave, a little of my heart will be left behind. Cuthbert and Aidan have become my companions – they are spurring me onward, bidding me persevere in my 'journey', especially when the going is tough.

Thursday, 22nd February

Looking forward to seeing my Sister later! Can't wait to share my joy with her . . . having discovered such a 'jewel' as this Island set in the Northumbrian coastline. Thought it would be overcast this morning in preparation for more wintry, colder weather, but, as always I was in for a total surprise – yet another beautiful day!

After completing a few household chores, I made my way to St Cuthbert's Island – constantly attracted to this small island. Thought I would be able to spend some time on here talking with Jesus, but looked at the approaching waters and decided only to stay some minutes. Wise decision! Very soon afterwards this island was cut off by the incoming tide. I sat on a cliff edge high up, and watched the waters close in. Delighted to see a few curlews on the beach. Just after spotting them a gaggle of ordinary and orderly Brent geese flew overhead. Whilst sitting on the cliff's edge, shared a little of my heart with the Father – I wish my mind were not so active!

Friday, 23rd February

Ten years ago today I made my bridal commitment. This morning I have thanked Jesus for his faithfulness and love; without him, I wouldn't be here now as his bride. Whilst praying it came to me that it doesn't matter where I am at, spiritually, in the present, perhaps compared with any of my Sisters – it all hangs on Jesus' choice of me. He has chosen me – I did not choose him. It has nothing to do with me. It has everything to do with him, 'who loved me and gave himself for me'.[12] Therefore, I can be at peace, and rest in his choosing and calling of me. I am happy that I am his bride, and he will complete what he has started in my life. The emphasis must always be on my Beloved – on Jesus. He must become greater and I must become less.

Wonderful, changeable, stormy seascape today! The Farne Islands, the Castles (Lindisfarne and Bamburgh) kept on disappearing in the storm and then reappearing just as suddenly.

Saturday, 24th February

This afternoon the snow fell! The Castle disappeared and then the thick snowflakes came tumbling down. It is exceedingly pretty – now that it has ceased snowing. The menacing, stormy look only lasted about half an hour. I like the snow-clad Castle.

Sunday, 25th February

How lovely the snow looks! The frost has 'glued' it to the earth. Intercession cross-stitch complete! A first for me!

Monday, 26th February

Opened the curtains to thick snow and still falling!

After lunch the fresh sea air and the wild winds beckoned. Stood for a while on the Heugh overlooking the Priory and St Cuthbert's Island. Cuthbert spoke – well almost! – in the vein of 'Be strong'.

Attended Evensong – at its close, whilst standing at the door, David Adam produced a carrier bag ('with things in it!') from beneath his black cassock! A gift of some beautiful Celtic cards! He is exceedingly fatherly.

Tuesday, 27th February

Worst snowfall in ten years, also snow blizzards. Apparently the worst northern gales for many years! Was awakened at 4.00 a.m. by tremendous gales. The mighty North Wind in full throttle! Awesome! I felt as though I were in a boat on rough seas. No sleep after that. No electricity. The waves by the Castle are exceedingly high. Very dramatic setting! No contact with the outside world. No reception on my little Walkman. We thank God for the oil-run Aga.

It is 9.35 p.m. and still no power. Writing this by torchlight! Day spent mostly huddled up to the Aga. Tea, supper and worship by candlelight. Jesus, the hearts of two lovers met in you tonight. It was special to worship together. I felt you were smiling at me while we sang: 'You are all my righteousness' – something has happened in my heart, Jesus, may it take root!

Wednesday, 28th February

More snow – still no power! The Aga and ourselves have become firm friends!! Plenty of laughs by candlelight – move a few inches away from the Aga and we could potentially turn into icicles! It is that cold. Can't really see what I'm writing – torchlight not that brilliant. The snow lies deep – a silent blanket – comforting like the blanket of Jesus' forgiveness.

Thursday, 1st March

Well, I can't leave the island, as planned today. More snowfall during the night. Snow hasn't lain like this here for 10 years.

Most roads – including the A1 – are impassable, so I'm enjoying being able to celebrate St David's Day on Holy Island! The first daffodils have opened in the glorious sunshine which we have this morning, so hauntingly beautiful this morning . . .

We have power! It was restored to us at 6.50 p.m.! Thank you, Father! It's been a tough few days. Many little and valuable lessons learned. Night prayer by candlelight.

Saw another lapwing pottering around in the snow earlier in the field in front of us. Two rabbits were leaping in the snow too – wonderful!

Friday, 2nd March

The enormous pool in the field in front of us has turned into a skating area – the blackbirds are fairly agile skaters! I sat alone on the Heugh for a while – 'My Trysting Place' – I shall miss this . . . saw some beautiful swans on the marshland near the causeway bridge en route to Berwick. Holy Island, in the distance, looked like an Icelandic Kingdom, on the return approach. Snow and blue skies make everything look so scintillatingly beautiful.

Saturday, 3rd March

Have decided to leave tomorrow . . . and the Lord has promised to go with me (thankfully!) Daily Light: 'My Presence will go with you, and I will give you rest.'[13] I do feel rather homesick too.

Elevenish – I'm sitting on the Heugh, watching the waters – the diamond pathway on them, created by the sun. By the harbour en route, I saw a few different species of birds together – seagull, two lapwings, oystercatcher, bartailed godwit and curlew. Father – how amazing is your creation!

I would like to continue memorising St John's Gospel when I am home . . . and reading Watchman Nee . . . and doing my cross stitch in the consciousness of His Holy Presence."

Friend Alongside

"We are not bound by any special relationships apart from our love for the Lord. This sets us free to love each and everyone with his special love."

As well as her practical duties, preparation for Bible studies and singing, another area of responsibility which God gifted her with was that of being a "friend alongside", or to use older phraseology, "the cure of souls". Sometimes when guests come to the house they ask for a chat or a prayer. As more and more visitors spent time with us it was inevitable that Lynda became involved in this work. It was only possible because she had grown in Christian maturity herself. She had learnt much through her own spiritual journey and living in community.

Moreover, she was perceptive, observant and discerning when it came to others. She had learnt to love others but not become over-emotionally involved however much a person was clinging to her for help. It is sometimes thought that we lead a sheltered existence. Nothing could be further from the truth. Lynda was not easily shocked, a necessary quality, as we listen to the appalling stories behind some lives. She was comfortable waiting in silence until someone was able to open up and did not rush in to fill the gap. At least one person expressed to us her appreciation of Lynda's ability to sit in silence. She understood and was sympathetic but could be firm when needed.

One day a full-time worker in the church arrived who was seeking spiritual direction. Lynda was the only one who was free. This lady had been hoping to see one of the older Sisters and refused Sister Lynda simply because she was younger. Lynda, whose time was precious, was undismayed by this, but that caller will never know what she missed! Many others have been grateful for Lynda's wise counsel and understanding heart. Sometimes it was a one-off chat and prayer but other times it was spiritual direction given over many years. "Lynda supported me through some dreadful times," one lady told us. Others wrote appreciatively of her "encouragement" and "guidance" and another of her help through "dark days".

Sometimes she would accompany someone on one of the many beautiful walks close by, listening and giving wise advice or encouragement. Teenagers responded to her. When one arrived to stay who had serious eating problems she was able to help her when many experts had failed. It was the turning point for this young girl. There is no doubt that one of the qualities which enabled her to come alongside youngsters with problems was that she wasn't afraid to apply firm loving. She listened to the Holy Spirit and his wisdom.

She often kept in touch by letter. Many treasured her letters. "Lynda supported me through the death of a close friend and wrote me many wonderful letters, many of which I have kept. All her letters were punctuated with God's words." "Most of all I cherish her letters," said another. An email arrived when Lynda was ill, "Your friendship has sustained me through some very dark days. After my return to the States your letters were so precious."

She learnt to love the unlovely – those from whom her natural self recoiled. Speaking of a time when she was younger, she wrote:

I remember one incident at the front door. I opened it to a young man, a down and out, homeless and wanting accommodation. Of course, we have to be cautious and discerning being a community of women but my immediate reaction to him was not a compassionate one. God used this incident to reveal the hardness and lack of mercy in my heart. But God gave me another opportunity later, to make amends and to show mercy. We began to have regular visits from a homeless man, Peter. He called once a week for his little chat and sandwich pack.

She started to make sandwiches for Peter, often including something special. Her chats with him were probably one of the highlights in his alcohol-sodden life. It came to an end when we heard one day that he had been found dead. There was genuine grief when Lynda heard the news. She never after that withdrew from those who had hit rock bottom and were living rough. The young men who came around the doors selling household goods found someone who was always willing to buy something from them, as well as listening sympathetically to their stories. Yet at the same time she remained discerning, quick to spot inconsistencies in what was being said. There was nothing sentimental about her loving.

She spoke about compassion flowing effortlessly when she was with patients at the cancer centre and visitors who came to the house, but the struggle was with those closest to her. She knew that this was the "acid test". So it is for all of us.

I can only share from my own experience – what a terrific battle I have had to be merciful when I have been wronged. In retrospect I am so thankful to God for the situations where anger and resentment have come towards me over the years, because my very reactions revealed a heart which was, basically, merciless, unforgiving and touchy. Time after time in the face of a wrong, I was aware of coldness, a withdrawing or a fear in my heart towards the person. There was no love and no pity. This in turn made me cry out to Jesus – at the end of myself – "Give me your merciful love."

Something has happened in my heart. Jesus has begun to soften it, to make it tender like his – perhaps he has sown the seed of his mercy there – he has had mercy on me in my mercilessness and lack of love. I pleaded with him for years. So he works in our hearts to make us more and more like Jesus. When I think about this miracle, it encourages me in my present battles because Jesus digs deeper into our hearts, as we journey on with him. Revealing more sinfulness – needing his cleansing, transforming power.

She became a friend to those who were enquiring whether they had a call to be a Sister of Jesus Way. One such wrote to her, "It has been extremely helpful to have you alongside me in my quest for guidance over these past months. Thank you for letting me open up to you and thank you for accepting me as I am." As Sisters joined us they found a friend in Lynda who was able to listen and advise them. This was because she had followed the Lord with all her heart and listened to His Holy Spirit, the Spirit of truth, in her own life. We cannot take others further than we are ourselves. We don't use the title "Novice Mistress" in our community but that, in effect, was what she became. It happened not by a vote in a meeting but by God's choice.

All the same attributes came to the fore – sympathy, understanding and firmness. She seemed able to deliver the truth in love with such a disarming smile that she caused no offence. At other times she had no qualms about gathering together Sisters where relationships had become strained. She would demand a fellowship in the light. In these situations there was a natural authority and for one who by nature was fearful, she was quite fearless.

It Is Being a Child

"When we live in simplicity we become childlike. Jesus said, 'I tell you the truth, unless you change and become like little children, you will never enter the kingdom of heaven.'[1] We are not cluttered by possessions and wrong attitudes. Our hearts are detached and free. We begin to see what is truly necessary and what is not. We are happy to let the latter go."

As Lynda approached her forties, still looking a youthful thirty, much of the intensity of her early Christian life had fallen away. "We always commented how she had grown in the Lord and saw such a freedom in Christ as the years went by," wrote a visitor who had first met Lynda in the mid-80s. "I never got to tell her," wrote another, "but she influenced my life so deeply, to love Jesus with all my heart and life just like she did."

Speaking in Lent she said –

We can ask ourselves, what beautiful thing can I do for Jesus, this Lent – in the midst of the darkness of this world and the busyness of life. In our Lenten Retreat we considered how we could draw close to Jesus, give him our love – talk less, stop and listen, less clutter in our rooms. Mine was to light a candle – ponder briefly on his sufferings – sing him softly a love song – "for when one sings, one prays twice."[2] Our hearts can be a Bethany, for Jesus.

Alongside her love for the Lord Jesus she became increasingly aware of herself as a beloved child of the Heavenly Father. Often, as we shared together in our lounge, and sitting in her favourite position on the settee, she would say as the conversation flowed, "It is being a child." It was this simplicity that enabled her to embrace responsibility in a way she could not have done when she was younger. She was made a trustee of the Sisters of Jesus Way in 1998. This may sound onerous but actually our Trust Meetings are happy occasions. It was, however, a further measure of the responsibilities she was undertaking.

The Heavenly Father led us into the Church of England in such a way that we were hardly aware of it happening! We had begun our life together as a community in the Methodist Church. Some of us will always be indebted to that denomination. Our formal ties gradually weakened over the years. This began when we drifted into an evening service at St Mary's, Upton – an evangelical Anglican Church. A Swiss helper wanted to experience lively worship and we had heard about this church. When she returned to Switzerland we continued to worship there on Sunday evenings. We were Methodists in the morning! We felt at home at St Mary's. Despite being an evangelical church with no more experience of Sisters living in community than Methodism, they accepted us without question. They began to pray for us and support us in many small ways.

We found on several occasions when we were facing a crisis, someone from St Mary's happened to be in the right place at the right time! Once it was an outpatient hospital appointment. One of the nurses said to us, "Haven't I seen you at St Mary's?" She strengthened us in the Lord. Later she told us that the pathologist for the clinic on that day was also from St Mary's. Similarly, we met a planning officer. He asked the same question, "Haven't I seen you at St Mary's?" Later, when our nerve was beginning to fail in a particular situation, he spoke bracingly to us about the meaning of Christianity, i.e. that we must expect opposition. It was a rebuke we needed.

Over many years we gradually drew further away from Methodism. Moreover, we now had Sisters who had no such link and when it came to church background we were a real mix! Finally we went onto St Mary's Electoral Roll and ceased attending the Methodist Church. At that point some within

Methodism pleaded with us to remain. It was too late. As we relinquished our membership some of us had to resign as local preachers. Friends were hurt and we were sorry. However, Brian Galliers, the Methodist Minister who had been alongside us since our first faltering steps in community and whose advice we valued, encouraged us.

Lynda had come to faith in Methodism and it would always be part of her. She delighted in an old book, *Anecdotes of the Wesleys*.[3] The anecdotes rejoiced in such titles as, "John Wesley and the Providential Shower", "John Wesley and the Ship upon the Rock", "John Wesley and Poor Louisa". There was ample scope for Lynda's fertile imagination when she read them and she repeated them to us laughing, and yet admiring John Wesley's calm imperturbability in every situation, the exact opposite of herself. She also loved a video of his life and we watched it many times. It inspired her. The well-thought-through doctrine of grace in Methodism ran like a golden thread through the community, as did the Wesleys' emphasis on holiness. Alongside Songs of Fellowship we sang from a Methodist hymn book. As we approached midnight each New Year's Eve we solemnly made our vows to God and still do, using an older version of the Methodist Covenant Service. Sister Divina, a Lutheran, said to us that John Wesley would be praying for us in heaven! We believed her. Lynda was by nature a contemplative but she also had a robust faith. Some of this was from her spiritual heritage in Methodism.

Brian Galliers, our friend and mentor, was concerned about our future and had brought up the question on several occasions. There was a choice: we went out on a limb or we became committed to a denomination. As we looked to our future the word that was beginning to focus our thoughts was "accountability". We had heard of some disastrous situations in both communities and fellowships when there has been no answerability. There have been particular dangers when leaders have become a law unto themselves. Our danger was not being fully committed to any denomination, or half committed to the Anglican Church and the Methodist Church.

Although we are more than sympathetic to the house churches and the independent fellowships to which many of our guests belong, we have always felt that it was right for us to be in one or other of the historic denominations. The question was: which one? We delayed.

There was a renewed sense of urgency when Brian, the dear Methodist minister and friend who had accompanied us for 28 years, unexpectedly collapsed and died in June 2004, not long before our 25th anniversary. We had voluntarily been accountable to him. He had been alongside us for many years. We could talk with him, share our accounts, seek his advice – and now he was no longer there. Most communities have someone from outside themselves who is called a "visitor" and we were now left without anyone. His unexpected departure to heaven left us isolated. We still couldn't see the way ahead clearly, although we realised the need. Accepting God-given authority, and correction if necessary, is the safest place to be. We knew this – but with whom was another question.

The Lord knew our need and he answered in an unexpected way. A short time after Brian's death, the Bishop of Chester paid a rare visit to the small daughter church of St Mary's called the Centre. As far as he was aware, there were no Sisters in his diocese and he was somewhat surprised to find some in his congregation. He sent a verbal message to the community saying that if we invited him he would be happy to visit us. As soon as that message came we knew that God's will for us was going to be the Church of England. Thus it came to be. A reply was sent in the affirmative.

On 31st October 2004, we celebrated our 25th anniversary as a community. We gave thanks for the leadings of the Lord over the past years and celebrated the goodness of the Heavenly Father. This had been truly miraculous. Close friends joined us. It was a wonderful anniversary. Our guest speaker was Dr John Newton, a Methodist minister who had been Chairman of the District some years before our anniversary. He had been wholly supportive. He shared that he had had to counteract much criticism of us in the

Methodist District, which surprised us. We had been blissfully unaware of this, which shows how effectively he had shielded us. We realise now with hindsight that much of this was caused, as criticism often is, by jealousy. Nothing could disturb our joy that day. The following Saturday we had a second celebration. About a hundred people shared our times of worship and testimony on the hour, every hour from 11.00 a.m. to 7.00 p.m. All the Sisters took part throughout, speaking and singing. Exhausted but happy, we came to the end of our celebrations.

Less than four weeks later Bishop Peter stood on our doorstep. It was 8.00 a.m. The Sister who answered the door looked through the clear glass and saw a smiling face. She knew that here was someone we could trust. Early morning visits became regular occurrences over the years. We were impressed! It gave undisturbed time for Bishop Peter and for us before busy days began. We had prayers together and then chatted over a cup of coffee. We felt that he understood community. We showed him around our houses. He could hardly believe that he had not known of our existence, although some of his clergy came to us for quiet days. At his request we gave him every piece of literature that we had about ourselves. Although he didn't mention it, we realised that we were placing the diocese in a vulnerable position. We were worshipping at an Anglican church and if anything did go wrong, it would be the Church of England on which it would reflect. We were not anticipating anything going wrong but life can take unexpected twists sometimes.

Then, and at a subsequent visit, we explored the possibilities for the future. Bishop Peter suggested the option of our becoming a joint Anglican/Methodist community. We felt that this would only multiply the number of meetings. Before too long we were on our way to becoming a recognised Anglican community with the proviso that a Sister could have joint membership – in the Church of England and some other denomination. Without his help it would have been impossible, as beyond the bounds of St Mary's, we had very little knowledge of the Anglican Church. In some ways we were as surprised as everyone else at the path we were on but we did not doubt that it was God's guidance. It happened so easily and gradually that we were hardly aware of the Holy Spirit leading us. Afterwards we knew that he had. We did not choose to be Anglicans, it simply happened. If we are children of the Heavenly Father we can trust him with everything.

Some of our friends were anxious, suspecting a take-over bid. One friend said to us on the telephone, "You are not going to change, are you?" She was expressing what we knew others had been thinking. We wrote in a newsletter at the time, "We will remain your Sisters, exactly as you know us now with our way of faith, trusting the Heavenly Father for all our needs. The Lord Jesus is our Head and we follow his Holy Spirit . . . There will be the same laughter, singing and occasionally tears! The house and garden here will embrace you, as always, in the love and peace of God."

It was a momentous year in which Lynda shared fully. At the end of the year Lynda celebrated her 41st birthday. She wrote shortly afterwards:

To be 41 is utterly glorious – means one step nearer to being with Jesus, seeing his face, no longer doubting his love for me in all my failure and weakness.

We all agreed that it was the will of God that we become Anglicans and nothing has happened since the decision was made that has changed our minds. Despite this the Church of England was a culture shock. Some of our guests were even more confused than we were, not least over how to address a bishop. One attempted a deep curtsey, much to Lynda's smothered amusement. We were aware of the problems that the Church of England was facing but we had confidence in our own church, St Mary's, Upton, and the leadership there, and we trusted our bishops. Bishop Peter did all he could to help us understand the sometimes confusing world of church ordinance, very different from anything we had known before.

We had long discussions in the office as to how to address an envelope to a bishop. Who was a Rt Rev. and who was a Most Rev. and was there some other Rev. of which we were unaware? There was – a Very Rev. Who was a Venerable? Our friend Ricky who had come here for years was a Venerable! It had never occurred to us! There seemed to be a bevy of Canons around. Who were they? Who were the Rural Deans who lived in cities? It was all very baffling to those who spoke Methodist language, Chair of the District, the Super (Superintendent Minister), the Connexion, circuit, permission to sit down (ministerial retirement) – no doubt equally incomprehensible to the uninitiated.

Lynda came alongside with abandon as we took the path to becoming an Anglican community. With her keen awareness of life she enjoyed the new experiences that were coming her way. From a relatively bishop-free existence we soon seemed to be meeting bishops galore. Her agile mind was extremely useful on some occasions. Her spiritual formation had been within the Sisters of Jesus Way and we had confidence that she would not compromise anywhere anything that we held dear – and she never did.

We encountered those in the Catholic tradition within the Church of England, as most, if not all, of the communities are High Church. We had much in common simply because we were all communities. We admired their emphasis on the holiness of God, especially in worship, and wondered if those of us from the evangelical fold are too casual as we come before God. We appreciated the breadth of the Anglican Church. Lynda's humour bubbled over as she watched some of her Sisters, out of politeness, awkwardly and self-consciously genuflecting. She coughed her way through clouds of incense. On one occasion a friend who was an Anglican priest warned us "to take no notice of the fancy dress". Lynda approached someone in unusual apparel and asked him who he was. We had never seen anyone dressed quite like it. This was no church service; we were heading for a picnic lunch. He drew himself to his full stature and replied self-importantly, "I am the Bishop of [the place will be nameless!]." It was indeed a new world. She told us this story with great glee.

A friend wrote of, "her infectious smile and naughty grin". That described her. In some situations her humour was unstoppable and occasionally, so was her curiosity. The religious equivalent of, "What does a Scotsman wear under his kilt?" was, "How much hair does a nun have under her veil?" The opportunity arose to find out and Lynda in great delight relayed her findings to us.

We were asked to speak at a meeting of clergy wives in the bishop's house at Chester. We looked at each other in consternation and no one volunteered to go. Eventually three Sisters agreed and one of them was Lynda. The day came and we set off for Chester, becoming more fearful by the minute. The room in which we met did not help. Large portraits of bishops of old, resplendent in purple and red, solemnly stared down on us. This was a long way from church halls, Methodist chapels and even our own homely meeting room in Redacre. It did not help our nerves! It was even further from tea, biscuits and, if you are lucky, a ham sandwich. As usual, Lynda was enjoying the new experience and she was the one who kept most steady while her Sisters descended into paroxysms of nervousness. When she sang, her lovely voice filled the room.

We were grateful to the Lord for the many blessings that came our way. We had sometimes found it difficult when we came to commitment services, of which there are three for each Sister as she progresses, because clergy had not been available or willing to help. When the Bishop of Chester became our visitor, or Bishop Guardian, he came to lead each service. This was more than we would ever have expected from a busy diocesan bishop. To our astonishment, at one service, we even had an archbishop from Melanesia. Life was full of surprises. Lynda delighted in them all.

We had tried once before to celebrate Holy Communion in our chapel each week, relying on retired ministers, but it had fallen through. Now with the clergy from St Mary's and our local parish church, St Bridget's, willing to help, a weekly communion suggested by our bishop became possible. This nourished us spiritually. It was appreciated by many of our guests, as well. Other Anglican communities welcomed us. Our days of not quite belonging anywhere were over and we all appreciated the sense of stability that this brought. Last but not least, a much-needed constitution was written.

Our horizons broadened, as we met Christians from the Congo and were visited by the Melanesian Brothers and Sisters from the Solomon Islands. Two Melanesian Sisters stayed with us for a week and some Brothers joined them one evening. We were encouraged by the childlike simplicity of their faith – something that we find far too easy to lose. We were moved as the Brothers shared with us the story of the martyrdom of seven of their number. Yet we were conscious that God, in allowing this tragedy, had in some way granted them a great grace. There were lighter moments too: much laughter and singing from both our communities. One lasting memory will be, as the Sisters were about to depart, holding hands with them and singing, "We are one big happy family . . . God's family are we."

We were pleased to welcome an Anglican Benedictine Sister from the Community of the Holy Cross, although our hearts nearly failed us when we knew she was coming. What would the real thing, a nun from a traditional community, think of us? Moreover she had been their Novice Mistress for years. She loved it and we loved her. On one visit a Sister accompanied her from a different community. We were a sight to behold, sitting outside a café, talking non-stop one sunny morning, one attired in a long black habit, another in a modern grey habit and two of us in our blue dresses and headscarves. The dog, who adapts to most situations if it means a walk, completed the picture. In some ways it may seem strange that an evangelical community should draw close to a community in the High Church tradition but our unity comes from our love for the Lord Jesus and His way of the cross. This transcends any differences in worship and theology.

In many ways for Lynda these were the happiest years of her life. Other Sisters had joined us. Now she was able to share much of the cooking. Although on Sunday mornings she was sometimes tired she still loved to sing for the patients in Clatterbridge Centre for Oncology. She felt at home on the wards. Visits to Holy Island continued to bring her joy. Most of all, she appreciated the love and friendship within the community. "Laughter in our midst," she wrote in her diary. Our meals were a long way from being silent, apart from breakfast, which was a more sombre affair! We chatted and laughed, enjoying our times together. In addition she had two new nephews, Ben and Jamie, who she adored. She was good with children. She was kind and understanding with a sense of fun.

Visitors, Hammers and Bricks

"There should be fluidity and adaptability; a will surrendered to God moves with the flow and direction of the Holy Spirit."

We believe that life is never static for a community obedient to the will of God. Change directed by the Lord is a sign of life. Every year brought new guests and consequently new situations. There were those who were afraid of our docile dog, and by that we mean terrified. A visitor, encountering him on the terrace, in terror burst through a locked gate leaving Thomas gazing after her in bewilderment. Persuasion was needed with some that arriving "early evening" did not mean at 11.00 p.m.! Special diets for medical reasons we could manage, but Lynda was not inclined to give in to fussiness even for a short time.

After we heard someone casting out demons on the upstairs landing, we wrote a note to be placed in each bedroom requesting those who were in ministry to leave that behind when they were here, and meet with the Lord Jesus themselves. Then we had saintly folk apologising to us that they had prayed with someone when of course, we did not mind at all! Only the wisdom of the Holy Spirit and a sense of humour brought us through many situations. Lynda excelled in both! We did not need to leave the house to experience humanity; the rich tapestry of life was presented to us, day by day. Letters, telephone conversations and emails furthered our contact with what soon proved to be a growing spiritual family.

This family eventually brought us into contact with persecuted Christians for whom we had prayed for many years. In 1998 a letter arrived. A sheet of blank paper had carefully made the contents unreadable through the envelope. The letter said, "Grace, mercy and peace from our Lord Jesus be with you. I have heard of your faith in Christ Jesus and of the love you have for all the saints,[1] which have been encouraging me. I always remember you in Jesus. Please pray for me, a China Brother." Three years later, in 2001, another letter came. This included the comment, "I think you know I have a little inconvenience here." Also, "I don't cease to remember you before my Lord these years." We have also prayed faithfully for him to the present day. More recently a Chinese friend who was staying with us told us that on a recent visit to China, he had met Jonathan (his English name). His comment was, "He has no fear. He will witness to Christ anywhere."

North Korea is the country that tops the list for persecuting Christians. A few years ago, Lynda answered the phone. It was a Sister asking if she could visit us and bring the pastor of the Korean Church in Manchester. A link was established. The minister was later grateful to be able to bring his leaders. On another memorable visit the church took over our kitchen and we all ate a Korean meal. Of greatest interest to us was the fact that the church members were from South Korea and North Korea. We met Christians who had managed to escape from the land for which we prayed earnestly. You can't book a flight out of North Korea, as someone who met them here mistakenly thought. It is a dangerous, fraught journey and for those caught, the consequences may be death. We couldn't quite believe that North Korean Christians were here in our home.

We were invited to the church for a special anniversary. A few Sisters, including Lynda, sat at the back of the church with headphones on, as the service had to be translated. It was difficult to remember that we were in Manchester! None of us would ever forget the hauntingly beautiful songs, cradled in suffering but simple and trusting. The words spoke often of heaven. The Christians in North Korea do not look for martyrdom but they look death in the face and they are ready. Heaven is a reality for them in a way that it is not for us. They sing of "his [Jesus'] companionship until heaven" and "there are no tears in heaven". The North Korean church see internment in prison camps (where there is torture, ill-treatment, starvation rations and harsh labour) as a continuation of their missionary calling. "I will continue my missionary work," as "I do not fear; the Lord is with me." It is impossible for a church such as this to die. They have counted the cost and are willing to pay it out of love for the Lord Jesus.

We heard the heart-wrenching sobs as an update on North Korea was given and the prayers that came from hearts that had been broken. There are, it is believed, 40,000 to 60,000 Christians in labour camps. That is a conservative figure. It may be as high as 70,000. If a Christian is arrested the family also go into the camp, including young children. Many of them die there. They are not allowed to raise their heads (to heaven). Eventually their spines begin to crumble.

After the service, which lasted about three hours, we were honoured guests at a celebration meal complete with a cake that Lynda, with another Sister, cut. There were long tables piled with food most of which we had never seen in our lives. Our new friends were anxious that we taste every Korean delicacy. As soon as we hesitated, wondering what something was, it was helpfully deposited on our plates. Lynda, who always enjoyed any new experience, loved every minute of being with these Korean Christians.

We have had Iranian pastors visit us who have shared first-hand the suffering of the church in their country. We were approached by a Christian charity in Manchester which reaches out to asylum seekers, asking us if we could help in any way – the obvious one was a day out by the sea. Lynda's immediate problem was what to give them to eat! Some were Muslim and others, Orthodox Christian. The latter, because of the culture in their country, ate similarly to those under Islam. However, the day came and all were safely fed without a problem. Inspiration came when we remembered a big tin of sweets that had been given to us. They soon disappeared. Afterwards, a few Sisters, Lynda included, accompanied them to the beach. This gave her the opportunity to listen to their stories. One was the only survivor from a massacre in his village. The Orthodox believers gave us insight into the persecution that they had faced. Later we were able to provide a quiet space for the same charity to bring those who needed trauma counselling.

Many were well educated and dear, dear people. The appalling treatment most had received in our country was nearly unbelievable. It was a revelation to us all. Scripture has much to say about the treatment of aliens in our midst. "He defends the cause of the fatherless and the widow, and loves the alien, giving him food and clothing. And you are to love those who are aliens."[2] It is easy to be influenced by the popular press and helping asylum seekers is never going to be a vote-winner. As Christians we are different, we think differently, speak differently and act differently. Our God has commanded us to love the alien amongst us. Some are our brothers and sisters in Christ.

We have learnt much from those we have met who are from the persecuted church. They love and forgive. They keep faith with the teaching of Christ. There is no bitterness or desire for revenge, only a desire that their persecutors will be saved by the Lord Jesus. These churches have nothing, as we would see it, but they have everything that is needed in Christ; whereas we have much but lack their riches in Christ. The persecuted church is cradled in suffering. Their priorities are prayer, evangelism, grounding new believers in the Bible and loving the Lord and one another. Lynda's faith, along with that of her Sisters, was strengthened by these contacts that the Lord gave us.

We have been encouraged and inspired by guests who are quietly living heroic lives for Jesus in their own particular situations. Our spiritual family grew as some visitors returned to us year on year. Correspondingly, the names on our intercessory prayer list also increased. We pray faithfully for those who request our prayers. We try to keep in touch with twice yearly newsletters. We would not have believed, if told when we started on this journey, where it would lead. By word of mouth, as we still never advertise, there are visitors coming to us from the far ends, not only of this country, but the world. Lynda was very much part of this – welcoming, listening, praying and loving. She had the best memory of us all. When someone visited us after many years, remembering us all clearly, while we were floundering trying to remember, it was often Lynda who recalled the guest. We were grateful to her!

We often receive thank-you letters and cards from those who have found peace with God in our home and met with the Lord Jesus. Sometimes we have been able to pray with them but often in the stillness and quietness they have met the Lord themselves. Sometimes we have had what we considered to be minimal contact with a visitor, yet we have been thanked for the love that they experienced from the Sisters. We can only think that in some small way the love of Jesus was in the house and we are profoundly grateful for his grace.

Some of the weekends that we lead ourselves have become firm favourites. Undeterred by rain, intrepid walkers arrive every year to join the Sisters on a Walking and Praise Weekend. Amidst the beautiful scenery on the Wirral songs of praise to the Creator ring out. Another retreat that has proved immensely popular has been the Quiet Weekend. Gently led through by the Sisters, there is no talking. In the silence there is opportunity to listen to the Lord. We are always full at New Year, a time of celebration, teaching, music and yielding ourselves afresh to the Lord as we step into the unknown. In much of this, Lynda participated with her music and teaching. She witnessed in her life to the Lord Jesus who she loved, although she was wholly unaware of this and would probably have denied it. The one thing about which she could be intolerant was false piety. No one could ever accuse her of that. She was who she was.

The ministry here necessitated many changes, as the years went by, in both the buildings and the contents. We were able to replace most of the second-hand beds in visitors' rooms. At the same time we laid new carpet, hung new curtains and bought fresh bed linen. On 8th March 2003 we gathered together and prayed in every bedroom. As was usual with us, part of the simple liturgy was sung.

Lord Jesus, in your Name we dedicate this room.
In the strong Name of the Holy Trinity,
We encircle this room with your holy angels.
We make the sign of your cross that the Evil One may never enter.
Lord Jesus, fill this room with your light, your love, your peace.

Let the light of the Lord come down.
Let the love of the Lord come down.
Let the peace of the Lord come down.

We pray for all who will stay in this room in the future:
Heavenly Father, shelter your children from all harm.
Lord Jesus Christ, comfort with your beloved Presence;
Gentle Spirit, anoint with hope and joy.

We bind unto this room today,
The strong Name of the Trinity,
By invocation of the same,
The Three in One, and One in Three.[3]

In 2006 downstairs rooms for visitors who are disabled were created and a large area beneath the house made suitable for storage. The alterations in Bethany were more major as an extension had to be built. In addition we built out to create a larger dining room. In subsequent years we made a number of rooms in Redacre en-suite. We are grateful that the Lord enabled this work to be done. In the middle of a building project it is hard work and sometimes there is anxiety but when it is completed and all the bills paid, we are full of thankfulness to the Lord. Although Lynda was not heavily involved in the practicalities, she had a keen eye for attractiveness and for that which looked right. She appreciated that beauty, God and peace go hand in hand. Ugliness or (she would add) untidiness are not part of his Kingdom.

We have been blessed with kind workmen always willing to go the second mile in helping us. The builders who we first employed in 2006 became friends. The boss makes us smile when his emails come, with the closing words "lots of love" followed by two kisses! You could say we have a relationship of trust rather than contract! Our plumber hurries to help us when the heating breaks down; likewise our electrician when electrics fail. Endowed with Liverpudlian humour, which seems to extend to the Wirral, they would pause when they met Lynda, for a bit of friendly banter and laughter.

There is seemingly never-ending new legislation regarding Fire Precautions, Health and Safety and Environmental Health. Some of this was directly Lynda's concern, especially Environmental Health. Legislation kept changing on Charity Accounting and Gift Aid. This also came under her remit. We looked back ruefully to the days when we began; it all seemed so simple then. Even in the practical situations that have seemed the most challenging and where we have felt (rightly) that we hadn't a clue, the Lord has led us through. He is a loving Father concerned not only with our souls but our everyday life.

In other areas we moved forward. We used a cumbersome and quite heavy paper diary that we carried from house to house, the problem being that it could not be in two houses at once and was often in the wrong place. We changed to an online diary that is available for us to use wherever we are working and especially tailored to our needs. The Sisters learning to use it has been another matter! Similarly, in this age of electronic communication we needed a good website. We now have thousands of hits every year. We have endeavoured to glorify the Lord Jesus in the web pages, encourage holiness of living and obedience to him. Lynda's mother tells us that Lynda reported all that was happening, excited at each step forward.

In the midst of this, one special visitor arrived on loan to us, so to speak, from the Heavenly Father. Lynda's joy overflowed when on Wednesday, 8th November 2006, her grandmother came to live with us. "Nain came to live with us today! Thank you Father for answered prayer," she wrote. We all loved Lynda's gran and she settled into a downstairs room in Bethany. She was 96 years old, frail but mentally alert. Lynda was 43 the following month.

The Dearly Loved Ones

"Jesus said to Peter three times, 'Simon, son of John, do you truly love me?' The questions to Simon Peter were followed with the words, 'Feed my lambs', 'Take care of my sheep', and, 'Feed my sheep'. [1] *Our call is not to Christian work as such but love for the Lord Jesus Christ. Our love for him compels us to a life of good works and merciful acts."*

Lynda's singing had opened the way for our introduction to the local Cancer Centre in 1993. The Heavenly Father has taught us the wisdom of following. God's work done in our own strength, and ahead of God's will for us, can have disastrous consequences. It is only when he opens a door to serve him in a particular place, or in a certain way, or both that we see this as his call. Sometimes the doors that he opens lead to a work that has been a secret calling in our heart for many years. Thus it was with Lynda.

It all began in a very small way, as often happens when we are being led by the Holy Spirit. We didn't see it, at the time, as the beginning of anything. Two ladies came to the house as day visitors. Both of them later became close friends. Paula, one of the two, was having treatment for cancer. We had already had our first brush with this illness within the community. We understood the shock that such a diagnosis can bring. The Sister concerned was aware of the need for sensitive and loving support for cancer patients. She made a point of chatting with her.

When Paula was admitted to Clatterbridge Centre for Oncology, often abbreviated to CCO, she decided to visit her. The following Sunday morning, Lynda was keen to accompany her. Quite unwittingly they were forming a partnership that was to last many years. It seemed a good idea to take some music, as Paula loved to hear Lynda sing. We arrived rather self-consciously on Mersey Ward, Lynda grasping her guitar and bag of music, for what was to all intents and purposes a one-off visit. After asking permission, which was readily given, she sang in the bay where Paula was a patient. Lynda's sweet voice and gentle guitar chords carried up the ward. A staff nurse, who was passing, lingered to listen. Afterwards, she asked whether it would be possible for us to come every Sunday morning.

That was the beginning of a ministry that was to bring blessing to hundreds of patients over the years. It did not begin the following Sunday. There were visits to the Nursing Officer who was in charge. She was in favour but had doubts whether everyone else would be. However, she encouraged us and suggested that "we give it a try for a few weeks". Our first Sunday morning some doubtful nurses were not sure about this innovation and, strangely, we weren't welcomed by the hospital chaplains, one in particular opposing us outright. Barriers came down with staff on the wards when we mentioned that we had been given permission by the Nursing Officer and they agreed that Lynda sing wherever patients wanted to listen.

We were nervous, as we ourselves were not certain what the reception would be. The patients loved it and loved her. The nurses too, as we went in Sunday by Sunday, were listening as they went about their work. Many of them loved it too. Years later, it was the Church of England chaplain, Rev. David Nugent, who brought us officially into the fold. Sister Lynda became what she had really already been for years, a volunteer assistant to the chaplaincy – with a badge to show it.

Another Sister made attractive bookmarks on her computer with comforting words and inspiring pictures. We took them in with us. Whole sets would sometimes disappear into pyjama pockets, always the men's! Sometimes, as we arrived on Sunday morning, patients were sitting outside, glad to be in the fresh air. We would stop and chat. Then Lynda would give them an impromptu concert before she went on the

Lynda, a 3-year-old at Penycae.

Lynda with long curls at 8 years old.

At 10 years of age Lynda was at Coedpoeth.

Morgan Lloyd school, 13/14 years old.

Lynda, 16 years of age with Hans, a puppy.

Setting off for Hull university.

Lynda as a student at Hull university.

Rev. Brian Galliers M.A., M.Th., our friend and mentor for many years.

We moved into Redacre in Febuary 1985. Stuart Macaulay was then our architect.

Our first community house in Lang Lane, West Kirby.

Our friends, Mason and Nora Porter, who were instrumental in the provision of our first two homes.

We began a self-build house in 1991 with much help from Colin Jones, our architect and Ronnie Fernihough, a builder who stepped in to help us.

Lynda as she went into our blue dress.   First commitment.

Early days in our community with our first dog, Benjamin.

Sister Lynda with Sister Divina at her Bridal Consecration in February 1991, "the happiest day of my life".

Sister Lynda cutting her cake, "beautifully made by my mother".

Sister Lynda with her parents after the Bridal Service and before supper.

Working on the building of the new house and chapel.

Our Motherhouse, Bethany, and the Chapel of Adoration were completed in 1995.

Lynda loved flowers, especially roses.

She was gifted as a flower arranger.

Lynda was gifted musically and played several instruments but her favourite was the guitar.

Recording our first CD in the studio of Tony Roberts.

A day out at Loggerheads country park. A well-deserved cuppa after a long walk.

Lynda with her family on Nain's 100th birthday.

Our Community as at 2009.

Our Community with Bishop Peter and Rev. Dan Paterson, Chair of our Trust.

The Dee Estuary from our garden—a view that Lynda loved.

A favourite place—Hobthrush or Cuthbert's Isle, off Lindisfarne.

wards. She loved the Liverpudlian humour that we met. Frequently it was the men who loved to tease her and make her laugh. One old man, much to the dismay of his more "respectable" relatives sitting around his bed, said to her, "You are a bit of all right!" He then looked at the much older Sister who was with her and commented, "And you are not bad, either!" Light and happiness seemed to follow us. Sometimes new patients were waiting for her. They had been told that a singing nun visited the wards on Sundays. Great was the disappointment when for some good reason we could not go.

More than once, a patient who had been asleep thought that they had arrived in heaven when they heard what they thought was the voice of an angel close by. Some took a little bit of persuading that it was not. Lynda would assure them that heaven would be even more beautiful, the voices more lovely. Often there was a round of applause after a particular song and comments such as, "You should be on the telly!" Lynda had no doubt that, given a choice, she would rather be singing in the hospital. It was a privilege. Occasionally we met another musician who fully appreciated her music. When a patient asked to play her guitar she would hand it over. Their skills were varied and we had some incredible renderings of anything from opera to the latest pop music but there was laughter, the illness forgotten if only for a brief time.

Occasionally we heard second or third-hand how much it had meant to a patient. A lady in our church shared, "A friend of ours was very ill in Clatterbridge and spoke of a nun who came around the wards singing – what a privilege it was to hear her – he wasn't Christian, but it made a deep impression on him because it was done out of love and not to raise money." Many patients reached for their purses, a sad indication that this is the association they have with the church. Yet their generosity was quite touching. We battled Sunday after Sunday, as we refused to take their cash. They were astonished at anyone refusing good money but it gave us the opportunity to say that we had a Heavenly Father who looked after us. The few strong-willed individuals who would not give in and forced a coin into one of our pockets were triumphant!

Many times there were tears, as the beauty of the music and the singer touched chords in lives that were anxious and taut. As the last echo of her voice faded, she would slowly take her eyes from the guitar, as if the music had held her in its grasp. It reminded the Sister who was with her, of artists she had seen perform in classical concerts. It wasn't only her voice that equipped her for this ministry. She was sensitive but not emotional, able to empathise but not fall into pity that would have been destructive. She was sensible, knowing when to speak and when to stay silent, who to approach and who not. Above all she was gentle. As one patient remarked, "Gentleness is in short supply these days." She was also able to articulate clearly her Christian faith when asked. Even her Welsh came in useful, as we sometimes encountered patients from Wales. She would sing to them in their own language and then talk to them in Welsh. This was comforting as some of them were a long way from home and their own culture.

Latterly she composed songs with the patients in mind – compellingly beautiful, gentle, encouraging and hopeful.

Before she left a bay she always sang a blessing. Often these, too, were her compositions:

Now may the Lord of peace Himself give you peace.
Now may the Lord of peace Himself give you peace.
Peace at all times,
Peace in every way,
Peace at all times,
Peace in every way.
May the Lord of peace be with you.
May the Lord of peace be with you.[2]

The steady, calm rhythm of the music embraced the words. The atmosphere perceptibly changed, as the peace of God descended on those who listened and it became, for a brief moment, "holy ground". There were many grateful patients. Some became our friends. One patient expressed it this way: "Sister Lynda, whose life shone light into my time at the Cancer Centre." Another wrote, "Thank you, Lynda, for having portrayed to us all the voice of an angel." It was by this that she became known in the hospital: "the singing angel".

Lynda's heart was in this ministry. She often spoke of a "call within a call", especially when she was alongside those who were dying. There were many who Lynda loved dearly and for whom she sang at the very gates of heaven. Sometimes she sang gently to them – songs of heaven and hope. Occasionally, we went into St John's Hospice and were welcomed there but we always felt that our calling was to the Cancer Centre. Our visits to the hospice were because we knew one of the patients.

As Lynda was a gift to the patients, they too were a gift to her. You can't race around a hospital ward, as she was tempted to do in other situations; it slowed the pace for her. Then there was the gift of the patients' love and the inspiration of their lives. She comments in a Bible study that she gave:

> I feel as though I have seen Jesus smile at me many times on the wards through the tender and grateful smiles of very sick patients.

One Sunday we met Alan from Skelmersdale. It was a meeting of heart, mind and spirit. He was a musician and loved the Lord Jesus. There was an instant rapport. When his visitors arrived, later in the day, he could not stop talking about the Sisters he had met that morning. His widow, several years later, visited the community. She brought with her a letter her husband had treasured, written by Lynda, dated 8th June 2009:

Dear Alan,

Please find enclosed a copy of our 'history', plus the music for the Holy Island Song and the Aaronite Blessing. We hope that each of them will be a blessing to you.

It was a real joy to meet you and to share with you. Your witness to God's love and goodness has moved us deeply.

With our love, and prayers, and every blessing. S Lynda.

Only a month after this letter was written, Alan went home to the Lord. It had given him joy to receive it. Lynda had kept her promise to send the music.

Our ministry to cancer patients opened up in another direction. Rev. Dr Pat Nickson, the Associate Vicar at St Mary's, was an innovator. When to everyone's dismay in 2008 she was diagnosed with a cancer that was terminal, instead of circling around her illness and herself, she used it to help others in similar circumstances. She also hoped that by sharing, with those who were well, her experience of approaching death, it would enable them to empathise in similar situations. Thus it was that she approached us and suggested that we start a support group. Before long four of us met together one afternoon, two Sisters from the community and two who were terminally ill with cancer, one of them being Pat herself. That was the beginning of a remarkable group that still meets twice a month. The two Sisters listened with amazement, as Pat and Angela laughed and joked about their funerals.

Lynda never lost her love for those who have cancer and she became part of the group as soon as it started. She brought her guitar along and often closed the gathering with one of the beautiful songs that she sang on the wards. We gathered a small group of those who, still on regular check-ups, were recovering from the disease. With their understanding of the illness, they became the nucleus encouraging those at the beginning of their treatment, giving friendship and pastoral care. The group is rather like a bus that some board for a time. Some board it and the illness is successfully treated and they return to working life. Others come to the terminus and step into heaven.

As we are Christians, we have a different take on cancer and a different take on death. We can pray together and for each other. The love and support is real and deep. There is understanding because we have all been there. One of the difficulties with cancer is that sometimes others are afraid, and, in trying to say the right thing to the person who has the disease, say the wrong thing. The cancer patient who is already feeling vulnerable may find this hard to take. There may be a conspiracy of silence in the family. It is truly a blessed relief to come to a group where there is openness, acceptance and freedom to laugh or cry. There is more laughter than tears.

We have been a very mixed bunch over the years. Cancer is no respecter of persons; it affects rich and poor, professional folk and those who work with their hands. Our group, which we later renamed "Cancer Friends Together", reflects this mix. In many ways, this illness is a great leveller. There has not been a hint of intellectual or professional superiority although sometimes members of the group have shared on such diverse subjects as abstract art (puzzled faces all around!), our legal system, social work and life as a policewoman. We have afternoons where those directly involved in working with cancer patients come to speak. These are invaluable and we are grateful to all those who have come – nurses who are proficient and up-to-date with the latest drugs, a radiographer from the CCO and a social worker from there. The chaplains have visited and a doctor from the hospice. The Christmas dinner followed by carols, and the summer cream tea on the terrace, are already firmly embedded in the tradition of the group.

Possibly the greatest good is done in small informal conversations at either the beginning or the close of the afternoons. Fears are expressed and news from recent appointments or results of scans, shared. Often a question arises, "Did this, that, or the other happen to you on chemotherapy?" There is nothing quite like talking to someone who has been there and understands. The only problem is motivating people to go home at the close! There is a reluctance to part.

The lives of many in our group have been inspirational. Inevitably those who remain most firmly in our minds are those who have now gone home to God. We have been privileged to know them. We were apprehensive about the first death in our newly formed group. How would this affect us? Would those recently diagnosed find it difficult? We need not have feared. In many ways it strengthened our faith and the group. Among the first of our group to die was Pat Nickson. One unforgettable moment for us, as we sat beside her at the hospice, was the visit by another member, Stuart. He was also terminally ill with cancer. He sat beside Pat and said, "Pat, I am so happy for you, you are going to a wonderful place."

Pat had expressed a desire to die with us. That proved impossible but we stayed with her at the hospice along with her close friend, brother and our vicar. It was Lynda, guitar in hand, who quietly and gently sang one of the last blessings prayed over her. The words are taken from the ancient Aaronite Blessing. Lynda composed the melody:

> The Lord bless you, the Lord keep you
> The Lord make his face to shine upon you
> The Lord make his face to shine upon you
> And be gracious to you
> And be gracious to you
> The Lord be radiant with joy because of you
> The Lord lift up his countenance upon you
> And give you peace
> And give you peace
> And give you peace.[3]

Because cancer is so prevalent, it should not have been surprising that some of our friends joined us. Ronnie was the young builder who had helped and advised us when we did our self-build. Now in his early fifties he was terminally ill but, wherever he went, his infectious faith was inspiring. Even in the operating theatre he talked about Jesus. He had lived much longer than expected. The day before he died he insisted that he check the electrics for safety at a large Christian youth gathering. He went home the next morning and died. We aren't all the same and our personalities don't change as death approaches but the grace of God for each one can make us "more than conquerors".[4]

When the time of our testing came, we were strengthened by the example of those we had seen who had trodden this path before us with faith and courage.

The Road Winds Uphill

"Let me be employed for you or laid aside for you, exalted for you or brought low for you."[1]

Lynda spent her 46th birthday on the 30th December 2009 in bed with a bad bout of flu, but she was full of thanksgiving to the Heavenly Father. She wrote in her diary:

> Ill on my birthday but the Father has overwhelmed me with his love, so many blessings! Beautiful cards, mobile phone calls and texts. Daffodils from my Sisters and an email from Sister Dorothea. My Sisters sang happy birthday to me this a.m. from below and again this evening – with two fresh cream cakes – one with candles on. An unforgettable birthday! Thank you Father. Special birthday Psalm, "God is our refuge and strength, an ever present help in trouble, therefore we shall not fear."[2]

She also found help from the words: "Confess your weakness to God, turn to his never failing love, and above all else, never mistrust his help."[3] She notes – "Will try to take these words to heart."

On 31st December, as the community, with their guests, committed themselves to God in the solemnity of the Covenant Service in the chapel, Lynda dedicated her life afresh to him in the quietness of her own room.

> I lit my candle in my room and read through, prayerfully, the covenant service making my commitment to Jesus, to the Father, to the Holy Spirit. I was so aware of the Presence of the Trinity and the mercy of the Father in forgiving my sins for Jesus' sake.

The previous few years had not been easy for Lynda. Her beloved gran had fallen and broken her hip. Despite her advanced years she had come through the operation that followed. She remained in hospital for almost three months. Lynda visited conscientiously, one step behind the nurses, applying the rigorous hygiene standards that she had set in our kitchen, determined that Nain would be well looked after. It was indeed fortunate for Nain on a number of occasions that Lynda was there. When it became obvious that her gran would never walk again and would therefore need 24-hour care, Lynda was involved in numerous meetings over funding. Although another Sister always accompanied her, she had to be the advocate. She ably discussed her grandmother's future care with an array of professionals from doctors and nurses to social workers. It was a great relief when funding was secured.

Alongside this she was visiting nursing homes near to us, ascertaining the best one for Nain. Returning from a disappointing visit to a home where there were no rooms available, Lynda decided almost on an impulse to try Westhaven Nursing Home in Hoylake. We had already heard good reports about this home. She knew as soon as she walked in the door that this was the place, but would they have a space? They had one room vacant. It was secured that morning subject to the Matron visiting Nain in hospital. Lynda never regretted that decision. Despite a traumatic discharge from hospital in an ambulance bus, when poor Nain was driven what seemed to her like a journey to the far end of the world, but actually was all around the Wirral, she arrived at Westhaven. Lynda was there to greet her.

Lynda lived with a fear of her gran dying. She said to one of her Sisters, "When she goes to heaven, part of me will go with her." No doubt her Welsh nature, attuned to melancholy, did not help and neither did her vivid imagination. Her fear dimmed in the busyness of every day. With our guests she was her smiling self, but it was always lurking in the background:

It is a strange thing on the one hand having to be so pragmatic, practical, purposeful, and on the other hand – these undeniable feelings of pain and anguish at an imminent loss.

I am a little fearful because various Sisters will be away over this coming month on Holy Island. I would like us to be together for Nain's funeral.

Nain had no such fears. When a terminally ill Pat Nickson visited her in Westhaven and suggested that they might both be in heaven soon, Nain replied, "Great!" Even Lynda had to admit, now and then, that despite fragile appearances her gran was "a toughie".

She had an even greater fear that her gran would die when she was away herself and it was with some difficulty that we convinced her that she had to have a holiday from time to time. Similarly we had persuaded her to allow us to visit the nursing home every other day so that she could have a break. We were missing her in the community. Lynda's parents, living in Wrexham, visited whenever they were able. Nain had been in Westhaven nearly two years and was rapidly approaching her 100th birthday. Her death was still uppermost in Lynda's mind in the first days of 2010.

(Preparing for Nain's passing into heaven) "Why should we weep for those who will never weep more, whose tears God has forever wiped away? – But faith certifies us that we shall soon be reunited to those whom in our earthliness we call lost – you will find her again in our common centre the bosom of God."[4]

It is difficult to understand why Lynda, who was so sensible with others, indulged this fear in her mind. Despite our entreaties to take a day at a time and that God would give the grace when it happened, she never managed to turn away from this, at times, quite crippling preoccupation. It was only when she was ill herself that she finally entrusted her gran into the care and keeping of the Heavenly Father and let go.

For years, visitors, hearing the Sisters sing, had asked whether we had recorded a CD. The time had never seemed right. We began to put out feelers, not quite knowing how to proceed, but they came to nothing. Then a couple from Liverpool, who we had never met before, came to stay with us. They heard us sing once in our morning prayers. As they were leaving, the husband, Tony Roberts, commented to the two Sisters in the entrance hall that he had a recording studio and we should record a CD. One of those two Sisters was Lynda. The Holy Spirit gave us a sense of urgency and an inner certainty that the time was right. With two composers in the community we knew that we would be able to use our own compositions. Songs were gathered together. Where copyright permission was needed for words it was sought and, within two months, in January 2010 we were ready to proceed.

For some time Lynda had said that she was unable to sing some of the higher notes that previously she had managed quite easily. With hindsight this should have been a warning sign to us. It passed us by. Lynda herself didn't see that there was a significant problem brewing and she needed help. The week before the CD was to be recorded the four Sisters concerned met to rehearse. Lynda threw herself into the singing, heart and soul. It was too much. There was already some slight residual voice strain and she was recovering from a flu virus. Her voice strained badly. It was a devastating blow for her. The CD was recorded with her beautiful guitar music and Lynda singing quietly. Although much can be done to boost a voice with modern recording equipment, she was understandably not happy with that. We decided to wait until her voice recovered and she could go back herself.

We hoped that a stay on Holy Island in February would give her the opportunity to rest her voice. It was as if everything worked against her. The Aga, which had plodded on regardless during all our previous visits, broke down. She comments, "Smoke billowing from the Aga – extremely fumy."

Never one to lose her head in a crisis she dealt sensibly with the situation but it involved phone calls and as anyone who has lost their voice knows, the telephone can be a problem. She concludes:

> There is a great temptation to believe (and desire) that holidays/retreats (especially on Holy Island) should be pure paradise from beginning to end – and how dare anything mar/destroy unbroken bliss! – but that is not "reality" – such times as these (and life itself) are/is dotted with glimpses of glory (of paradise) and these glimpses of glory are seen on the way of the cross – the one and only way to which I/we have been called while I/we tread this earthly path. This is the way of the cross, sharing the darkness – and my Father has blessed me with wonderful glimpses of his glory – foretastes of his paradise – during my days here on this beautiful Island. Oh Lord Jesus, may I truly walk this way of the cross in my heart (not simply in my head).

Back home in West Kirby she notes, "Voice worse but the Father knows and he has encouraged me." Some words from her earthly father struck her as being from the Holy Spirit. "Be patient," he had said. He knew her. Patience was not one of her strong points. Problems multiplied. Nain was very deaf. For years Lynda had had to raise her voice when talking to her. This too had probably played its part in damaging her vocal cords. Thankfully her gran had excellent eyesight. She didn't even need glasses! Lynda began to "speak" to her by writing notes.

She missed singing, as she had loved it. Especially she missed singing at the CCO and her beloved cancer patients.

> I miss not being able to go there, but Father I give you my "yes", and bury my face in your heart.
> It wasn't easy not being able to go to the hospital (today) because I don't have a voice. However the word of God in

my Losungen [a German Devotional that Lynda used] was quite clear in that I must be "thankful always" and that I must "sing in my heart to God".

In mid-April she was still struggling with her voice. And in her diary she quoted two lines of poetry:

> "Thou hadst not 'that', my child,
> But thou hast me."[5]

The "that" being my place at the CCO.
I love you Lord Jesus. I am happy to be in your shade. You forgive me gladly and freely for my longings to be in another place.

Daily life is infinitely more difficult without a voice, especially when you are living with a group of people and visitors. Although we tried to shield her, it wasn't always possible, especially as we had two other Sisters seriously ill, one having major surgery and another, radiotherapy. Lynda's hopes would rise as her voice improved and then be dashed as it deteriorated again. In addition, advice given was sometimes conflicting:

> I've been given contradictory advice so sometimes I've not known where I stood!! "Don't stop speaking or your voice will seize up." "Whisper and whisper properly," "Don't speak." Then the registrar tells me, "not to whisper but to speak in a loud voice". You see and know it all Father.

This was eventually sorted for her when after many months she was given access to good speech therapists. Speech therapy continued for the remainder of the year, as both speech therapists that helped her were determined that her beautiful singing voice be restored. One of them had heard her singing in our chapel some years before.

Her fears increased not only over her voice but pain in her hip and back.

But it is important that I divorce/see the pain as separate from my fears – fear of what might be.

Another simple poem has also been helpful.

> "When the/my cloud of battle-dust may dim
> His veil of splendour, curtain Him
> And in the midnight of my fear
> I may not feel him standing near
> But as I lift my eyes above
> His banner over me is love."[6]

She found help in prayer and clung to the Lord.

> Thank you for your loving Presence, and although I am unable to speak to anyone else, I can pour out my heart to you, my loving Father. Thank you for your many gifts, and that I am far from being alone in this desert place.
> May you become my dearest companion in this isolation/loneliness which comes with not having a voice.

As always, she found solace in the beautiful world around her,

> Daffodils about to blow their trumpets!
> Glorious day today, walked on the Wirral Way – saw swallows, a greenfinch, skylark, peacock butterfly, comma, painted ladies – ladybirds on hawthorn – nature bursting into life. Felt uplifted, and was lifted up to my Father's heart!

On 30th May, she returned to the CCO unable to sing, as she had done formerly, but to talk to the patients.

Went to the CCO for the first time since Christmas – it's a step in the right direction and I felt as though I had come "home". My voice held out but it is uncomfortable now and weak. Father, I trust you.

In June Nain celebrated her 100th birthday, her granddaughter proudly by her side. There was a letter from the Queen. The Deputy Mayor, relatives, Sisters, care workers who were not on duty, arrived to offer their congratulations. Flowers arrived in abundance. There was delicious food prepared by the cook.

As the year progressed improvement with Lynda's voice was disappointingly slow. Her anxieties were increasing. Never a good sleeper, she felt a constant tiredness that was dragging her down. A Sister has a vivid recollection of her standing in the office, handbag under her arm, dark circles under her eyes, about to visit Nain – and her heart went out to her. Perhaps her final illness had already begun to take its toll, as it was to be less than a year before she went home to God. We were later appalled when the belt of a new dress came into our hands. We could not believe the smallness of her waist. As she was always slim, we had not noticed, but there must have been considerable weight loss.

She poured out her heart to the Lord:

I was sitting under our vine – talking to my Lord Jesus (I have felt so utterly down today) – telling him that He is a far more loving Bridegroom than I can imagine – that he bears me with gladness – "remembers my sins no more",[7] never regrets his choosing of me. (Sister Divina used to say those words to me). I heard him speak (in my heart), "Lynda, my dearest bride, have I not betrothed you to me forever – in steadfast love, in mercy and in faithfulness?"[8] His peace stole gently into my heart. I have hope despite this clinging weariness.

At the beginning of September she asked if Graeme would anoint her with oil for the healing of her vocal cords. She records in her diary:

The presence of the Holy Spirit was almost tangible as we prayed in the chancel of St Mary's Church, as Graeme made the sign of the cross on my forehead and on my vocal cords. The "liturgy" for the anointing was beautiful. So, my Lord Jesus, my voice in its brokenness has been given back to you, it has been consecrated to you afresh – and I look to you to restore it. For some time afterwards I truly felt (i.e. in the bank in West Kirby) that I had truly been set apart for God. Graeme said I would be as a "garment of praise".[9] And in the quietness afterwards he had the words, "Christus Victor" buzzing around his head. The Sister with me had a picture of the resurrected Christ-cum-Good Shepherd – with flowing, bright robes, carrying me, his lamb, in his arms effortlessly because I was so light.

Two friends gave us the use of their villa in Sardinia. In late September/early October when we knew it would be slightly cooler, Lynda travelled there with three Sisters.

Mountain air, pure! Scenery barren, desert-like. – North Africa not so far way. Cacti, fir trees, howling dogs!! First glimpse of the Mediterranean Sea lapping the shores of this southern part of Sardinia. Wonderful.

She loved the opportunity to learn Italian, experience new places and walk along the beaches, drinking in the beauty, and warm sunshine. We were concerned that she relax and gather strength. She was determined that she would have a go driving the car, which was left-hand-drive and right-hand side of the road, despite dreading this before she left home. Italians seem to change character once they are behind the wheel of a car so driving in Sardinia could hardly be described as relaxing. She writes triumphantly in her diary, "Drive (Yes!)

to Maracalagonis and back. Bought fruit and vegetables on roadside from our farmer."

She mentioned, once or twice while we were away, a pain near her left side but it didn't seem to be affecting her too badly. Lynda's body was as sensitive as her nervous system. We thought that this was another of the minor problems she had suffered throughout the years. We were aware, however, that she was more uptight and edgy, not herself. She was not well. None of us thought for a minute that it was anything serious.

A short time after we returned to West Kirby the pain sharpened. Lynda was sent for an ultrasound scan. It revealed a shadow in the left ovary. It was decided that she should have another ultrasound a few weeks later. This would reveal whether or not whatever it was in the ovary was growing. The pain, however, was increasing and Lynda was also complaining about feeling bloated in the abdomen. She also wanted one of us with her when she saw doctors. A Sister, who accompanied her to the GP's surgery, remembered uneasily all the posters that she had seen in Clatterbridge Centre for Oncology that said this was a symptom of ovarian cancer. The anxiety that was already there increased as she realised that we were possibly facing a life-threatening illness. The problem for the doctor was that the bloating could also be the symptom of several other conditions, at least one of which Lynda had had. The Sister saw the concerned look on the doctor's face, as she glanced in her direction, and knew that she was not alone in fearing the diagnosis. Lynda was referred to a consultant and the request for an appointment was marked "urgent".

"God, Me and Cancer"

"There is strength in our togetherness that is needed not only for ourselves but also as an encouragement for other Christians. 'A cord of three strands is not quickly broken.'[1] *We need each other. This is not a sign of weakness but of strength."*

Lynda also was beginning to have a suspicion that the pain could be an indication of cancer. One of her aunts had died from cancer at the early age of 47. The disease was prevalent on one side of her family. By now it was December, the month of Lynda's 47th birthday. She began a new journal on 12th December 2010. She later gave the journal a title, "God, Me and Cancer".

I asked the Lord Jesus for a word from him this morning, having told him that I am so afraid of impending hospital appointment and the mysterious pain in my left side. He heard my cry! The Old Testament word in my Losungen was from Zephaniah – significant in the German, "have a terminal illness"[2] (I fear cancer!). The New Testament word – "Jesus came and touched them (the disciples). 'Get up,' he said, 'don't be afraid'."[3] Even the prose below brought reassurance – "Dem suchenden Menschen kommt die ewige Liebe entgegen. Seinem Dunkel das Licht, seiner Unrast die Geborgenheit. Seiner Krankeit das Heil."[4] [Translation: Eternal Love comes to meet the person who is seeking. To his darkness comes light; to his restlessness comes security. To his sickness comes well-being.] Thank you, my Lord Jesus. "The Lord, the King of Israel, is with you; never again will you fear any harm."[5]

Throughout the last months of 2010 Lynda went about her work with her usual quick smile, refusing to burden others with her problems. She helped with the accounts and drove a Sister down to Shropshire. She visited the wards in Oncology and organised the Christmas dinner for our Cancer Friends Together. She helped cook and serve the meal. Her shock at the price of turkeys momentarily took her mind off her own difficulties! Her voice was improving all the time although she was still cautious about singing. Her Sisters were becoming more and more concerned. As Christmas approached we gathered together as a community and laid hands on Lynda.

My Sisters surrounding me, praying for healing. I still have pain but I am trusting in Jesus. There was such a sense of your presence, Lord, as we prayed at the end. My reading was from "God's Little Book of Calm".[6] "I will . . . make the rough places smooth."[7]

A Sister had also given her that verse when we prayed together. On 23rd December, she saw the consultant. He was a kindly, fatherly man who made her smile when he said, to her astonishment, "Did you enjoy your time in Sardinia?" She was still trying to figure out how he knew when he said, "I have my spies everywhere!" He was gentle, too, in other ways, trying not to frighten her. He thought the problem was the ovary and not elsewhere but he said, "to eliminate cancer" (as a cause of the pain) he would arrange for a CT scan and a colonoscopy. Blood tests were taken. We mulled over his words, as we recovered from the appointment, with a cup of tea in the cafeteria. "To eliminate cancer," Lynda repeated several times. That evening she wrote in her journal,

Special words given by Casper ten Boom to his son and wife – the Holy Spirit underlined them for me – "I believe what is happening to you can be compared to an oak tree which is being violently shaken by a storm, but which therefore reaches down its roots even more firmly into the ground."[8]

The pain was increasing. "I keep looking to my Lord Jesus," she said. "He shares my humanity, my pain. He became flesh and dwelt among us." Despite the pain she loved Christmas.

So appreciated the beautiful carol singing this Christmas – Handel's Messiah on Radio 3 (truly inspired), Classic FM carols and tonight Winchester Cathedral Choir. Truly – Christmas is a season for adoration – we adore our God, who in Christ became incarnate.

It was a white Christmas and the ground was frozen solid. We sang around our little Christ-child as the day began. The Christmas dinner was not without its hitches, one of which was the turkey. For some unaccountable reason, it went into the oven upside down! We fitted in a visit to Nain, singing Christmas carols in her room. A fire was lit in our dining room. As the day closed, we sat around the embers singing.

Thursday, 30th December 2010, was her 47th birthday. She writes,

A beautiful birthday despite the pain and inevitable underlying anxiety. The recurring promise throughout the day – an enormous encouragement: "For I know the plans I have for you," declares the Lord, "plans to prosper you and not to harm you, plans to give you hope and a future . . ."[9] It featured in several birthday cards. Began reading "God's Little Book of Peace".[10] Looked up the (Bible) reference and my eyes slid to the verse before it which reads, "But the Lord said to him, 'Peace! Do not be afraid. You are not going to die!'"[11] Amazing . . . Because the Lord knows my fears!

1st January 2011 was a Saturday, and we were full for our New Year's Celebration. Lynda helped cook a meal for 22 people. God's presence was in the kitchen. We could feel the peace. The Lord had given a beautiful word to us as a community. "My Lover spoke and said to me, 'Arise, my darling, my beautiful one, and come with me. See! The winter is past; the rains are over and gone. Flowers appear on the earth; the season of singing has come, the cooing of doves is heard in our land. The fig-tree forms its early fruit, the blossoming vines spread their fragrance. Arise, come, my darling; my beautiful one, come with me.'"[12] It was Lynda who remembered that this was a word that had been given to a Mary Sister we had known, when she was dying.

Her personal word, given to her on 1st January, was a word that spoke of the love of God for her. "The Lord your God is with you, He is mighty to save. He will take great delight in you, He will quiet you with His love, He will rejoice over you with singing."[13]

A few days into January the scan and a colonoscopy were imminent.

In the early hours of this morning, the Lord Jesus seemed to say (allaying my doubts and fears), I am the Lord of GRACE, and so, of course, I am near. I am close beside you. Beloved Jesus, you are here, close beside me. Precious words! If there weren't such a quality as grace, I would have every reason to doubt his love and his presence in this situation, as I await the diagnosis and alleviation of the pain, but alleluia, he is with me!

The day of the long awaited scan arrived, 6th January. That evening she wrote in her diary,

Thank you, Father, that the CT scan is done! Thank you, Father, for your "praying people", for a number of wonderful emails expressing great love and support.

"My heart is filled with thankfulness
To Him who walks beside."[14]

135

The same night she wrote:

Deep discussion with [one of her Sisters] about death and dying. When there is the possibility that we might die sooner. We all have to die at some point! This is the only time when we can do nothing other than yield ourselves completely to God.

The following Monday it was a colonoscopy.

"Therefore my heart is glad and my tongue rejoices; my body also will rest secure, because you will not abandon me to the grave"[15] (in view of awaiting diagnosis).
    The colonoscopy at Arrowe Park was an ordeal this morning. I felt terrific pain throughout. Afterwards I thought, "It was my little Calvary." (It was so painful I was crying out). Later, I reflected on the magnitude of Jesus' suffering for our redemption – a tiny glimpse into the pain of his crucifixion. None of us will have to go through anywhere near the sufferings he endured.

The procedure had been horrendous for her. She was sick as soon as she returned home. The Sister who had accompanied Lynda knew that the time had come to be pro-active and not sit back waiting for the NHS whose wheels were grinding slowly, when the nurse said to Lynda, "There will be an appointment with the consultant in a few weeks." A few weeks were too long. On their return she rang the surgery and asked to speak to our doctor. Our GP acted very quickly and within 48 hours we had an emergency appointment.

Wednesday, 12th January 2011
Emergency appointment with specialist nurse at Gynaecology Department, Arrowe Park. Appointment 1.30 p.m. (but owing to mistake, didn't see the nurse for another two hours!). Just after 1.30 p.m. – all of a sudden

– felt the Peace of God descend upon me like a blanket – and enter me – and I know it was the prayers of God's people. I am so blessed to have so many deeply committed godly people praying for me. I shall be "prayed" into wellness, or into Heaven . . .

In this appointment I was told I had cancer – a mass in the pelvic cavity (extra-peritoneal!) – one of the worst moments of my life, and yet a strange sense of relief and peace that the "waiting" was over . . . When you are told you have cancer, in a moment everything is different – nothing will ever be the same. I realise as never before the fragility of life – my mortality (and yet, in Christ Jesus, I am immortal!).

We were not actually told. The specialist nurse, obviously trying to find a way to cushion the blow, was using medical jargon neither of us understood. It was Lynda who interrupted her, saying in a voice verging on panic, "It's cancer, isn't it?" There was a silence, which said everything. She left us alone, with the door open for some air, as she went to find out the earliest possible appointment with the consultant. It was arranged for a few days later.

In the following days Lynda turned to her diary again:

What a beautiful verse the Lord Jesus gave me in "God's Little Book of Peace" tonight. "Then your light will break forth like the dawn, and your healing will quickly appear; then your righteousness will go before you, and the glory of the Lord will be your rear guard."[16]

Thursday, 13th January 2011
I have asked the Lord Jesus, "In these days please draw me to you, I want to be near to you. . . ." Have received many emails declaring love and support for me/for us at this time.

Friday, 14th January 2011

"My God,

I have never thanked Thee for my thorn.

I have thanked Thee a thousand times for my roses

But never once for my thorn.

Teach me the glory of my cross.

Teach me the value of my thorn.

Show me that I have climbed to Thee by the path of my pain.

Show me that my tears have made my rainbows."[17]

We were all concerned about Nain and the effect on her when she discovered that Lynda had been diagnosed with cancer. A Sister went to see the Matron at Westhaven. She felt, like us, that for the moment Lynda's gran should not be told and somehow they would get around it. The kindness and support of Margaret, the Matron, nearly caused tears to flow and a steadying cup of tea was gratefully accepted.

We had become friendly with one of the nurses, Angie, through our ministry in Clatterbridge Centre for Oncology. She no longer worked there but was still working with cancer patients. She had said to us that if we ever needed her she would come. She knew Lynda well. She came alongside us immediately. How thankful we were for her expertise, her sense of humour and her knowledge. Her favourite expression was, "Don't you worry, now." Strangely enough, when Angie was around, you didn't! She had soon roped Rose, another ex-CCO nurse, into helping us, too. Anxiously, the Sister who had accompanied Lynda each Sunday on the wards, at the next opportunity spoke to Gail, one of the nurses. "We will look after her," she said confidently. Suddenly all those years visiting that hospital, Lynda singing, were being returned to us a hundredfold, in love and understanding. But there were many miles to travel before we reached Oncology, and some without the care that we were later to receive there.

On Sunday, 16th January 2011 Lynda wrote:

"Say 'yes' to the will of the Heavenly Father,"[18] (very apt words in the face of my appointment with the consultant tomorrow). A little later in the morning a Sister came to my door with a verse, which after some deliberation, she felt was for me. Little did she know that the Lord gave this verse to me in the early hours of 16th June last year. It was as if God tapped me on the shoulder to make sure I was sufficiently awake to take it in! This was also the verse I had chosen as my "scripture to take with me into the New Year" – (session in New Year retreat) – not knowing then I had cancer. "And the God of all grace who has called you to his eternal glory in Christ, after you have suffered for a little while, will Himself restore you and make you strong, firm and steadfast. To Him be the power for ever and ever."[19] What an encouragement to receive this verse again this morning! Thank You, Father.

Angie, our friend from CCO days, who is a specialist nurse, said it would be a long road, and we would need to be prepared for this. Angie thinks the consultant will go for surgery first, and then chemotherapy – we shall see. YES, FATHER to your will, to your plan.

Just read next phrase in "God's Little Book of Peace".[20] I was amazed at the reference, "Weeping may remain for a night but rejoicing comes in the morning."[21] My eyes caught sight of some preceding verses (which I believe the Lord wanted me to see!) "O Lord my God, I called to you for help and you healed me. O Lord, you brought me up from the grave; you spared me from going down into the pit"[22] – another confirmation that I shall not die.

The day of the hospital appointment, Monday, 17th January, began early for Lynda:

It's 2.25 a.m. The pain is really bad and I can't take any more painkillers until after 3.15 a.m. I decided to read "Daily Light" for this morning. Again, my Lord, I am amazed at how you are "talking" to me through your Word!

The same verses as last night appear in it. I sympathise with King Hezekiah's questioning.

"In the prime of my life
Must I go through the gates of death
And be robbed of the rest of my years?"[23]

What a privilege to have Keith Sinclair, the Bishop of Birkenhead, talk with me, listen to me, anoint me with oil and pray for me this morning! At the end of the prayer time (with all my Sisters too) he felt he should share the words of Jesus, "I came that you might have life, and have it to the full."[24] I shared with him some of the scriptures the Lord had given. He said, "These are life words" to hold onto. He asked me if I had any fears, to which I replied, "Yes, the fear of falling apart." – He said it was allowed!! I said I needed much courage, and that I didn't want to bring any dishonour to Jesus.

At 1.20 p.m. (should have been 12.30 p.m.) we saw the registrar. He had to bring in the consultant. They can't tell exactly where the cancer is situated. My case has to go to the multi-disciplinary meeting on Thursday where consultant and radiologists will discuss the matter together. I am so grateful for a Sister being with me for the consultation, and another in the background. I have wonderful support. Please, Lord Jesus, help me to shed light and peace among my Sisters! It isn't easy for them. Help me so that I don't cast a cloud over everything.

Tonight read in "God's Little Book of Peace" – "The Lord will protect him and preserve his life . . . The Lord will sustain him on his sick-bed and restore him from his bed of illness."[25] – all about healing and restoration once again!

The community also was in a state of shock, swinging between hope that Lynda could be healed (there had been many promises not least to Lynda herself), yet knowing that her death was a very real possibility. We were trying to protect Lynda and she was trying to protect us. We were also trying to protect our visitors, many of whom come in need of rest and with their own problems. Thankfully, the day after this appointment we had no visitors. It was the mercy of God, allowing us time to meet together and to share our fears openly. We admitted that we all felt inadequate in the situation, were having difficulty not to fall apart, but we came back to the place of trust. We were children of the Heavenly Father. He would truly be our Father in our need. We trusted him. We committed ourselves to God and to being open and honest with each other. We even saw a few smiles. We were all, including Lynda, struggling towards an acceptance of God's will whatever . . . The same day Lynda confesses, in her journal:

> I have a prayer on my wardrobe door. It came alive for me this morning. All I can do in my position is yield completely to the will of the Father.
>
> "FATHER,
> I abandon myself into your hands;
> Do with me what you will.
> Whatever you may do, I thank you.
> I am ready for all, I accept all;
> Let only your will be done in me
> And in all your creatures.
> I wish no more than this, O Lord.
> Into your hands I commend my spirit;
> I offer it to you with all the love of my heart.
> For I love you, Lord, and so need to give,
> To surrender myself into your hands without reserve
> And with confidence beyond all questioning,
> Because you are my Father."[26]

The support for us all was growing, as more and more of our friends realised the seriousness of the illness. Lynda wrote:

A precious letter from Sister Mary Michael – I shall read it over and over again! A special gift from Father this afternoon – a 'phone call from Sister Divina!! I explained that the doctors would be meeting tomorrow to try to locate the exact position of my cancer. She replied, "But the Father knows – we will ask the Holy Spirit to show them!" Then she said, "I have a postcard near me, in my room, which reads (rough translation from the German) 'Prepare me in this short time (of life) to spend the whole of eternity with you. There, in eternity, there is no fear, only peace.'" I told her that I want to be prepared. I want him to prepare me. What joy to hear her voice.

"Prepare me in this short life so that I may spend the whole of eternity with you." The words echoed in her heart. Our dear Sister Divina, now 92 years old, came alongside Lynda once more. Earlier that day Lynda's parents had arrived. She commented, "Not an easy morning – seeing my mum and dad for the first time after being diagnosed with cancer. They were in pieces but gradually pulled round!"

We spent almost all the next day waiting for a telephone call that would inform us of the decision made by the multi-disciplinary meeting. They had chosen an operation with a full abdominal incision. The surgeon would be able to see exactly where the mass was situated and do a full hysterectomy at the same time. Various options had been mentioned at our previous consultation, but not this. It was not what Lynda had been expecting and she was shocked. "My Father, it's scary, but I trust in your love!"

In the days before the operation she turned to her journal again:

Sunday, 23rd January 2011

Appreciated sharing honestly with [a Sister] that I have no true desire to go to Heaven yet. She reassured me, explaining that it is quite a normal reaction because God has given each one of us a "will to live". Jesus is near, although I don't "feel" him as such. It boils down to (in these seasons of numbness and overwhelming) "naked faith".[27] Returning to the "heaven" theme – Jesus will "lighten" my path there, when it is my turn to "come to him".

Read the following extract – a booklet written by one of the Sisters at Malling Abbey following a diagnosis of cancer:

"There was an unforgettable ceremony in the old rite for the profession of a nun. The novice knelt at the back of a church while the bishop from before the altar sang, 'Come.' She rose and moved forward, singing, 'and now I follow.' A second time, on a higher note, 'Come: and now I follow with my whole heart.' A third time, insistently higher, 'Come,' moving up to the foot of the altar she sang, 'and now I follow with my whole heart. I revere you and seek to see your face. Do not put me to shame but deal with me according to your abundant mercy.'

"Part of the hundredfold of the monastic life in community down the years has been the opportunity to take leave of each of the old nuns after she has died. Laid out in the cowl in which she has for so long worshipped God, with the vicissitudes of the past transcended, the whole of her life and character can be seen caught up into the peace and majesty of death. This silent dignity leaves a deep impression on the mind and spirit. One cannot but be convinced that we are on a pilgrimage through this world and that our lifetime here is meant to reach a point of completion since the end for which we were created lies beyond. When God invites us to 'Come' all the way into heaven, what can we do but gather up our penitence and our hope, together with thanksgiving over our rich experience of the miracle of life, and follow with our whole heart?"[28]

Evening

"Hope" is the gift which must be rekindled in me after all this trauma and shock because "hope" is the quality which will set me apart from others, make me distinctive from those who don't profess faith in the Lord Jesus – amidst this crisis. I've just read this verse, "May the God of hope fill you with all joy and peace as you trust in him, so that you may overflow with hope by the power of the Holy Spirit."[29] I think this verse will stay with me and become a "reality" in me. I sense the Holy Spirit has underlined it for me tonight.

Monday, 24th January 2011

During a corporate time of "quiet" this morning I had a little picture of the Father running to meet me, as I approached him a little uncertainly from the opposite direction. He was trying to convey to me that he loves me dearly and wants to shower me with the 'hope' which I've requested – and the peace, and the joy. . . . He does not give begrudgingly, half-heartedly, but he lavishes his goodness upon me/us . . . and especially when his child is in great need. This is my Father! And it has nothing to do with my merits or de-merits, but simply because he is Love! Teach me, Father, to snuggle up to your feathers as I learn to take refuge under your wings . . . The waiting – now to receive a date for my big op – is almost unbearable. Father, I am trusting you to encase the cancer within me, so that it doesn't spread. The days are passing . . .

The next day there was a meeting of our Cancer Friends Together:

I broke the news at the Cancer Group that I also have cancer – each time I say it, it feels like a thunderbolt going through me – the very uttering of those words. People were extremely loving afterwards. I'm one of them now!!

144

A Sister drove Lynda to the estuary – her beloved estuary. They sat in the car and watched the winter sunset reflecting gold, sepia and orange in the still water of the marine lake, the birds bidding their farewell to the day. She cherished it.

She did not have much longer to wait for a date for the operation. It was to be on 4th February. A little practical diary she kept indicated that she was still organising much of the catering – "Defrost turkey", "Kitchen equipment, special offer for paper towels and pedal bin", "Begin frozen food list". She had the foresight to see that someone else would have to take over and there are little reminders as to what the other Sister must be told or taught. She was meticulously organised regarding her medication, washing of bedclothes and much else besides. Her visits to Nain had almost stopped and there is a note a few days before the operation to "write Nain a letter". Alongside this the cancer was taking its toll – "A very bad night – pain upon pain and nausea – crying out to the Father! Wanted to simply curl up and die!"

She was determined to stay thankful:

Thanksgiving
To be able to share with [a Sister] and for her prayer and reminder that I must let myself be carried by the prayer of others.

A Sister – bringing me two lots of toast (couldn't face anything else today).

Shafts of sunlight in an otherwise dull, dreary day – watched them from my bed.

Some miniature daffodils – hope of spring and resurrection.

Sleep last night after bad bout of sickness and therefore being unable to take the stronger painkillers – managed to take some paracetamol at midnight.

Thank you for Angie and Rose, our "chemo" nurses calling in.

Thank you for a Sister's tender care this morning – and simply being there.

A very kind pre-op nurse and for a Sister waiting with me and for me. Bless her Father for her love to me . . . and all my Sisters!

So many encouragements received today – an abundance of cards, emails, words of scripture. I am truly blessed. Jesus' gift to me today has been his "Peace" – a sense of calm.

Christine, whilst hoovering, asked the Lord for a word of encouragement for me, and there before her on a piece of card was the verse, "The Lord himself goes before you and will be with you. He will never leave you nor forsake you."[30]

My lovely downstairs room in Bethany where I cared for Nain up until three years ago. It is peaceful here.

She was very brave but she confessed that the week prior to the operation had been the worst week of her life. 4th February arrived. There was an e-card for Lynda from Sister Divina and Sister Elisa. Sister Pista, another older Sister, wrote to us from Darmstadt. She accompanied us throughout with her letters and prayers. That evening Lynda was attached to various machines, pale and dizzy. She was, however, fully aware and keeping an observant eye on everyone and everything. It was two days later that the blow fell. A text message came from Lynda, "Please come, as soon as possible." A Sister hastily went to the hospital. The tumour had been inoperable. It was encasing a major blood vessel. The surgeon had done all that she could, even calling in a vascular consultant while Lynda was still under the anaesthetic. Nothing could be done. They simply closed her up again. Two Sisters travelled to Wrexham the next day to break the news to Lynda's parents.

Angie knew the pain control team at the General Hospital, and she rang them. They also knew Lynda through her work with cancer patients so the pain was sorted immediately. Lynda too, once she recovered sufficiently, was her old firm self. She said quite bluntly that she was not going to be discharged until she had seen either the consultant or one of her team. A Sister spent hours at the hospital waiting with Lynda for this visit. We eventually saw the registrar. We said that we wanted some choice over which consultant oncologist Lynda was to be under. He saw no problem and explained that another member of the team would give us the biopsy results, as soon as they were available. To our utter dismay this other person proved exceedingly difficult.

Lynda arrived home but not before confessing to the Sister with her, as they walked down the hospital corridor that, "she didn't want to die". Lost for words, the reply came, "I don't want you to die either." Within a few days we were back for an outpatient appointment where we were to be given the biopsy results. One Sister accompanied Lynda and another Sister accompanied them both! Courage was failing on all sides. We knew this appointment was crucial. It was our kind registrar again but also the member of the team who had opposed our wish to be consulted about which oncologist. The biopsy results were devastating. It was ovarian cancer and clear cell. Lynda said to him, "Is that an aggressive cancer?" He replied, "It moves fast." This piece of shattering news was almost lost in the head-on clash over which oncologist. We gave the name of a woman consultant we wished to have. We were informed enigmatically that there would be a meeting at the General Hospital the following Thursday. In desperation, the Sister with Lynda suggested that if the male oncologist was "put out", they should say we wanted a woman. This was partly true. We also wanted someone who was sensitive and kind. It was a devastating appointment in every way.

In a piece of writing later published in St Mary's magazine, Lynda described the journey home:

As we drove home from this devastating appointment I caught sight of our beautiful, beloved estuary and I long to see it many times more but now there is a distinct possibility that I won't. That was followed by another anguished thought – if I go to heaven soon I shall have to wait a long time until I see my dear ones again and I don't think I can bear it. At 47 years of age I desperately wanted to live. There is nothing wrong in this. God has given us so many precious people to love and so many things to enjoy in life. They become even more beautiful and precious when there is the likelihood that they will be taken away. I was feeling a little guilty that I quite honestly didn't possess the burning passion/desire to go to heaven. That also is a gift of God, I'm coming to realise.

We had a gift in the afternoon. Bishop Peter arrived, solid and reassuring. He sat and talked with Lynda, and the Sister who had been with her that morning, about life and death, and being a child of God.

Lynda describes what it meant to her:

He is gifted in putting things clearly – theologically – I found his certainty in the resurrection (of the body) and life after death "rock-likingly" reassuring! He wasn't afraid to speak about death, my death. . . . He assured me, gazing at me most directly, that I would be given the grace to come through, and that I would be all right, whatever that might mean. He said, whatever our age, we are all children of the Father – 6, 47 or 70, etc., whenever we die, we die as a "child" of the Father. He also said that everything is preparation and nothing is an end in itself. Life is a journey to God. The very reason we are given this life is so that we can journey towards God. He felt sure that my sense of remoteness from God (shock) will lift in time, and that I will know him near, because he is very near.

Thank you Father for his strengthening visit and presence.

We all had night prayer with Lynda – she launched into a talk to the other Sisters that was excellent, quoting extensively from Bishop Peter. The next morning we had communion together.

All the Sisters were gathered in my room, and Graeme led it through. He chose as his passage – the raising of Lazarus – and looked closely at Jesus' question, especially to Martha – "Do you believe this?" Jesus said to her – "I am the resurrection and the life. He who believes in me will live, even though he dies; and whoever lives and believes in me will never die. Do you believe this?"[31] (I want to give my resounding "Yes! Lord, I believe!!") Apparently Edward the Confessor's last words were, "I shall not die for I am leaving the 'land of the dying' to go to the 'land of the living'."

I attempted to share some of this with Mum and Dad when they visited later in the morning. They shed many tears but I want them to glimpse something of the reality of eternal life and the resurrection of the body.

She was grateful for all the prayer around her:

Nora F. [Sister Nora Fowler] during her last night in hospital prayed for me throughout the night. As she recited "The Lord is my shepherd" she was given a deep certainty that I was cradled in the arms of the Good Shepherd, and he said, "I will take care of her." How special to learn that I am being prayed for in the Congo! Gill Brown and Elias both sent emails assuring us/me of their prayers. The Congolese certainly know how to pray because they have suffered.

Our next-door neighbour, who had been at Lynda's Bridal Consecration, has an upstairs room that overlooks our Bethany. She could see Lynda's bedroom window. Hilary and her husband, Jeff, would sit on the edge of a bed, their hearts breaking, as they looked down at our property. They held hands and prayed for her. That meant so much to us. Two communities came alongside us, the Anglican Benedictine Community of the Holy Cross and the Evangelical Sisterhood of Mary, especially their house, Jesus' Peace, where many of their frail retired Sisters, including Sister Divina, lived. There was more or less constant prayer from them alone, not to mention all our other friends. Many prayers, from countless people, and we were grateful.

Lynda again recalled her Bridal Consecration:

24th February 2011

A day of "variety" – this is how one could describe yesterday. 23rd February, 20 years ago I made my Bridal Consecration – giving my "yes" to Jesus to be His Bride. Many times I have been so unfaithful but he has overflowed in his faithfulness towards me. Polycarp's Day yesterday too – I felt his fatherly smile upon me.

She adds,

Jesus is saying – "You are completely and utterly 'known' (as St John would use the word – intimately). Do you believe this?" (Not do you feel it?)

About this time she managed to visit Nain for what was to be the last time. She took with her a letter she had written.

Dear Nain,

I am writing this down because I can't shout! It is wonderful to be able to see you today after such a long time! You are always in my heart and I have thought about you and prayed for you many times during each day.

My Sisters have been great in keeping an eye on you. I am sure you would agree. They come to tell me all about you each visit. You are special to them too. As you know, I have had a big operation and have not been so well afterwards. And now I am going to need further treatment and therefore I will not be able to come and see you often. I will try to come every few weeks if I am well enough. However, I always feel very close to you, and because we both believe in the Lord Jesus, we are together in His heart and nothing can separate us from His love. He is your Good Shepherd and He is watching over you.

Keep smiling, Nain!

With lots of love, hugs and kisses,

Lynda xxxxxxxxxxxx

P.S. I can't believe you are nearly 101 years old!

Lynda told us when she returned how loving the staff were at Westhaven. "Some of them kissed me," she said, obviously delighted.

A copy of the letter that had been sent to the GP arrived in the post. The results were more encouraging than we had hoped. It was still only primary cancer, but it was advancing rapidly. We did not recognise the name of the oncologist to whom Lynda had been referred. We rang CCO and no such doctor existed. One of the team from the General Hospital telephoned us and assured us that the referral, despite the wrong name, would have gone to the consultant of our choice. We were not so sure and soon discovered that the referral had gone elsewhere and then been passed on again. Our fear was that it had gone to the consultant that we didn't want. Eventually we contacted the secretary of the doctor we did want. We knew that speed was of the essence if Lynda was to be helped. At last we met someone who agreed! She arranged an appointment for the next day with the right team at the Women's Hospital in Liverpool.

Lynda describes the appointment:

First appointment with oncologist yesterday – a long, long wait, and a long, long appointment. Daunting, challenging, very slim chance of a cure with chemotherapy (this hit hard) – but prolongs life. Much suffering lies ahead. O Jesus, this is my Gethsemane – everything within me cries, "If it is possible, please take this cup from me . . ." But the Father is waiting for my "Yes". Hospital – cold, clinical, medical – and there I lose hold of the fact that I'm a child of the Kingdom of God. With God in the equation there is always hope! Encouraging New Testament reading this morning: "Are not five sparrows sold for two pennies? Yet not one of them is forgotten by God. Indeed, the very hairs of your head are all numbered. Don't be afraid; you are worth more than many sparrows."[32] I will lose all my hair very early on.

The chemotherapy was explained to us and Lynda gave her consent. It was planned to begin the very next week. We were glad when we arrived home but grateful that at last, Lynda was under a consultant at Clatterbridge Centre for Oncology.

The next day was beautiful and even warm. Lynda was able to walk gently in the garden that she loved. Then unexpectedly she collapsed. She later said to Angie that she would have been happy to die in the warm sun, with the birds singing and the spring flowers around her. It was not to be. The next day she was admitted once again to the local hospital with a blood clot and a collapsed lung. A Sister went with her in the ambulance but when it became certain much later in the evening that Lynda would be admitted, she had to leave her. To our dismay, when we visited, she told us that the previous night a doctor had said to her, quite brusquely, "You have cancer, so if this blood clot moves do you want to be resuscitated? – think about it." We were shocked at her being asked such a question, in such a way, and when she was on her own. It was a nurse who had said to her, "Of course you want to be resuscitated; the cancer is in its early stages."

Once on the ward all went well for a time. Consultants were kind and understanding, including one who liaised between the local hospital and the CCO. We were conscious that it meant that once more the chemotherapy was being delayed and humanly speaking, this was her only hope. It was an aggressive cancer. Anti-coagulant injections were started and these were to continue, one each day, throughout the chemotherapy. One of the consultants had a gut-level feeling that part of the blood clot had broken away and lodged in her lung and that this was the cause of the trouble there. He wanted a scan. A week had now passed. Nothing happened. We requested to see the nurse-in-charge and asked what was happening. She promised to find out. Nothing happened. The weekend passed and again on the Monday a nurse was approached. We were assured that it would be sorted – still no scan.

The Sister who was visiting Lynda the next day asked to speak to a doctor. Who should arrive but the doctor who had been thoughtlessly insensitive when Lynda was admitted. He was a smooth character. He spoke as if we knew nothing, avoiding the central issue, which was why they weren't getting a move on with the scan when the CCO were anxious to get started on the chemotherapy as soon as possible. The impression given was – "Why bother? She is going to die anyway." It was only the thought that one day this doctor would have to answer to God, that enabled the Sister concerned to have some compassion on him.

We now had to cancel Lynda's first appointment at the CCO. This alerted the secretary who had helped us once before when we were in difficulties with the local hospital. She contacted the hospital for us. Also, a junior doctor, who had been observing all that was going on, tried to help. This joint effort produced a result and the next day Lynda had the scan. There was a large blood clot on the lung and we were told that it would take a further three weeks to disperse. She was very breathless on exertion. Before she was discharged, another doctor arrived with an entourage. In the entourage was "the smooth one". The Sister with Lynda got up to leave the room but Lynda said firmly, "She is staying." She sat down again! The consultant knew us. It was a wonderful gift. "The smooth one" stood back, not saying a word, with what can only be described as an ingratiating grimace.

Lynda was discharged. District nurses began to come in every day. The doctors at the CCO didn't waste any time –

although she was far from well, it was decided that chemotherapy should begin within a week. News about Lynda was spreading. We decided to send out email bulletins, so that misinformation was avoided and those who loved her could accompany her in prayer. The first email was sent bringing a torrent of replies, all of which were relayed to Lynda.

The Singing Angel

"Thus shall I walk with Thee,
The loved Unseen;
Leaning on Thee, my God,
Guided along the road,
Nothing between."[1]

Lynda's first session of chemotherapy took place on 10th March 2011. It was impossible not to think of the many times we had gone through this hospital door, chatting happily, talking to patients we met and giving impromptu concerts on the way. In many ways we were back on "home ground" and we were grateful. We were overwhelmed by the kindness shown to us. There were willing hands to push the wheelchair, words of encouragement and practical caring. We met the consultant for the first time, although we knew her team had been active for some time behind the scenes. Lynda was on the drip for five hours and it all went smoothly. Her sense of humour came to the fore, as we tried to manoeuvre the chemo-stand on a visit to the loo. It went everywhere but where we wanted it to go. We giggled our way up the ward, full of admiration for the many patients we had seen doing the same thing, apparently effortlessly.

A week later, she wrote what was to be the final entry in her diary:

Friday, 18th March 2011

People think the "glory" is in the resurrection but it is actually seen in the cross – the glory is the "self-giving" love of Jesus on the cross to us.

Our "glory" is that we are "beloved sinners" – for we have received, believed in, embraced Jesus' self-giving love for us on the cross (which was his glory) – his glory enters us as we become one with him.

A thought from the Holy Spirit last night –
When the time "nears" for me to leave this earthly life (and it might not be too far off now), the Holy Trinity will draw near in love – the "Eternal" will become a far greater reality than the existent, earthly "present". I am therefore not to be afraid.
And the time is not yet.

Lynda's body reacted badly to the chemotherapy. It was only with the help of our ever-attentive doctors, the district nurses, paramedics who were kindness itself, an out-of-hours doctor who was also very kind and a 24-hour emergency phone line to the CCO that she made it. Angie and Rose were always there for us, encouraging and advising. Her hair began to fall out. She didn't bother with a wig. Instead we made a slightly larger headscarf for her and she wore it low down on her forehead, Mother Teresa-style. One of the Sisters made her a glamorous hat in our blue. We encountered a difficulty that was to occur many times. Many of the professionals had very little or no understanding of a Christian community. Our doctors were fine. They knew us well. We had a succession of district nurses and we felt that sometimes a boundary was crossed by some, when they asked Lynda questions that were inappropriate and unnecessary, and which she found distressing. Yet at the same time most of them said how much they loved coming to us.

Three weeks passed. She went for her second chemo-therapy, again as a day patient. Five minutes into it she had a severe allergic reaction and went into anaphylactic shock. Doctors came running from all directions. The Sister who was accompanying her thought that she was dying and Lynda thought the same. They brought her round but she was admitted to Sulby Ward. One morning, when she was feeling low, she thought, "Where are you Father?" She went to open a window. As she glanced out, a vivid rainbow formed. It remained there and she heard the Father whisper, "I am here, I am with you."

Despite her own problems she brought blessing to the other patients. All the gifts that had aided her on the wards came once more to the fore. A husband was visiting his wife in the next bay. Years of seeing her suffer had become too much for him. He left her bedside, possibly to leave the ward; instead he went to Lynda. He was angry and bitter. The words poured out of him. She simply listened and loved him until the torrent ceased. Perhaps she was able to say a few words. We don't know, but she gifted him with the peace of God. The patient opposite was Stephanie. She sent a card to Lynda, as soon as she was home: "It is so nice to have met you. You have been lovely company. It would be nice to keep in contact with you. Keep strong, lots of love."

Over the years, Lynda had met a number of hospital chaplains who were now patients. A number of them were in difficulty making the transition from helper to being helped. There were exceptions. Sister Helen had assisted with the Roman Catholic chaplaincy, but one morning we found her seriously ill in the CCO and later we visited her at the hospice. She was loved wherever she went both in chaplaincy work and, more importantly, as a patient. Lynda was the same. What made them so different? Possibly both had been schooled in humility and prayer so that it had become a natural part of their lives. In the most unconscious way Christ shone out of them and his light could not be quenched whatever the circumstances they were in.

We were constant in our visiting and text messages flowed backwards and forwards. Eventually an excited text came, saying that she could come home late afternoon. We did not delay and soon she was back with us. A few days later she returned for a further attempt at chemotherapy. She was nervous and so were we. The consultant said, "We will keep our fingers crossed." When Lynda promptly said, "And pray," she smiled and replied, "Everything." Lynda had been on two separate chemotherapies. Although they had to abandon the one, which caused the severe reaction, they went ahead with the other. Great care was taken. A cocktail of drugs was administered first, to forestall any problem, and the chemo was dripped in slowly. We distinctly heard the nurse say after two difficult stages had been passed, "Thank you, Lord." We silently said, "Amen."

Lynda no longer had the energy or the concentration to write but she was still able to read. The bookmark in her much-loved Losungen had written on it, "Life is a journey towards eternity and each day is a milestone along the way."[2] Her thoughts were more and more on heaven. She loved the words, "Now we live in the hope of eternal life because Christ rose again from the dead. And God has reserved for his children the priceless gift of eternal life; it is kept in heaven for you, pure and undefiled, beyond the reach of change and decay. And God, in his mighty power, will make sure that you get there safely to receive it, because you are trusting him. It will be yours in that coming last day for all to see. So be truly glad! There is wonderful joy ahead, even though the going is rough for a while down here."[3]

An old hymn was beside her. A pencilled line in it marked out this verse:

Before Thy throne we daily meet,
As joint petitioners to Thee:
In spirit we each other greet,
And shall again each other see.[4]

Bishop Peter came again, fitting us in after a meeting. He is a theologian. Lynda was a thinker, as against an emotional person. She liked to know/understand. It was the meeting of minds, as well as the unity in the Holy Spirit, that helped her, with his guidance, to face dying.

There was still laughter. She couldn't wait to tell us when something had happened to someone else that had made her amused. She was organised and in control of her drugs. Partly this was fear. She had heard of mistakes in the NHS and liked to keep an eye on things herself, as far as she was able. Gradually, as the chemo worked its way into her body, the side effects became more than she was able to bear and we could handle. She was advised to go back to the day ward for help. Early one morning she walked out of our back gate and into the car. Our neighbour, Jeff, was putting his wheelie bin out and came over. Putting his arm around Lynda he asked her how she was. "Not good," she replied. We drew away. None of us, least of all Lynda, realised that she would not return.

We arrived at a busy, bustling oncology centre. Lynda was grateful to be given a bed straight away on the day ward. It was decided that she should have a scan and be admitted. The porter arrived to wheel the bed to its next destination. We knew him. Once he was over his shock that it was Lynda, we set off at a brisk pace. Arriving at the Radiotherapy Unit we were met by Fiona, a Christian radiographer, who also knew us, having visited our Cancer Group. These familiar, loving, concerned people gave us the strength we needed and the assurance that the Lord was with us. A bed had been found for Lynda on Conway Ward. For some reason this had always been our favourite ward. It was here a few months before that a nurse had said, "We will look after her." The ward had only been open for two weeks, after extensive alterations. It looked very different. We were taken to the modernised side room that was state-of-the-art. Lynda was the first occupant.

Claire, a junior doctor, arrived with the results of the scan. She was friendly and kind but the news was devastating: the chemotherapy had not worked. The cancer was advancing rapidly and there was a new tumour on the other side of the abdomen. She left us. The peace of God descended on the room. We sat for a while in silence, not a shocked silence but the quietness that comes when you know a battle is over. Lynda said afterwards that she had felt the peace of God. She could feel His presence. He had spoken reassuringly, saying that everything would be OK.

Within a few days she was more comfortable, the more distressing symptoms under control. A blood transfusion brought new strength. Her sense of fun and humour reasserted itself. She told us of the hilarious time she had had with a nurse when, unused as they were to the new bathrooms in Conway, water had come spurting out where it wasn't wanted and stayed stubbornly unattainable in places where it was needed. She was moved to a bay, as a more seriously ill patient needed her room. We both smiled when a healthcare assistant who had returned to Oncology after eight years, stood at the foot of the bed, hands on hips, and said with a cry of delight, "I would have known you two anywhere, you haven't changed a bit!" That was a compliment indeed! Wherever we went in the hospital there were enquiries about her, the nurses who remembered her singing, the cleaners who loved her, the WRVS helpers with whom we had chatted and of course, the chaplain who knew Lynda well. There were even patients who recalled her beautiful voice. There was an unmistakable feel of a family around us.

At Redacre, the strain of carrying on as normal was beginning to tell and we decided to close the house to guests after Easter, which was then almost upon us. The extra office work sending out bulletins, keeping those who were close to Lynda informed and reading all the incoming mail was considerable. Some friends quite spontaneously sent us money to cover any extra expenditure. We were aware of the love and prayers of the Christian family surrounding us. Trusting the love of God each day and accepting his will sustained us.

A nurse rang late one morning, saying that Lynda wanted one of us, as the doctors had been round. The cancer was travelling faster than they could keep up. Their preferred option was no further intervention. Lynda agreed and she was grateful. The doctor came back, kneeling down and holding both our hands, explaining again what this would mean. A specialist nurse, Ann, accompanied her. There was a choice: Lynda could remain on Conway Ward, or go to the hospice.

When we realised that coming home could mean the local hospital if there was an emergency then that option was excluded. Lynda was concerned that if she remained on Conway, she would be taking a bed that someone else needed. Ann hastened to reassure her on that point. The nurses on Conway wanted to care for their "singing angel". We heard that they were quite touched when told that she wanted to stay with them. In the meanwhile, Ann caught the Sister who was with her, for a brief minute or two, and warned her that Lynda could die quite suddenly. They didn't know.

Lynda was moved back into a side room. Photographs were brought in for the windowsill. A new notice board was soon filled with cards. In the centre we placed a beautiful picture of the cross on St Cuthbert's Island, Lindisfarne, and beside that the well-known statue of St Aidan who first brought Christianity to Northumbria – precious gifts from our friends on Holy Island. There was always a flower or flowers from our own garden beneath it. We continued to bring in emails each day. Some of the most touching were from Janet, a member of Cancer Friends Together. Seriously ill herself, she wrote:

If you think that Sister Lynda would like to hear this, please tell her that, having been closer to the "pearly gates" than some others, I am drawing strength from her certainties about what lies ahead. Please give her my love.

Our Lord's times are not our times; and I still draw strength from Sister Lynda who is treading a path that I may follow in the not too distant future.

We were about to have lunch one day when a text arrived from Lynda. "I am ill today." It was her Gethsemane hour. A Sister hastily set out for the hospital. There was a noticeable improvement almost as soon as Lynda saw her. She began to talk and shared that she felt that the peace of God was like the sea. The surface may be stormy but if you go down far enough then it is still – that despite all, she still had the peace of God deep down. Praying especially the prayer of simplicity (simply being in God's presence) she touched the calm beneath. She struggled with the thought of leaving us. One evening, soon after this conversation, she broke down. She was going to miss us. One of the older Sisters said, "It won't be so long until I am with you." "That is nice," she replied and sank back on her pillows.

A nurse was inspired to go and ask the Sister in charge of the ward if we could bring in Thomas, our dog. She was soon back. We could bring him in, as often as we liked, as long as we kept him on the lead! Lynda's face lit up as she confessed that she wanted to feel his soft fur one more time. Playmates for a brief moment were reunited. She lovingly ran her fingers through his thick, black coat. Once was enough; she said her farewell to him and we didn't take him in again.

Her thoughts turned again to our beautiful estuary. "I would like to walk on the beach one last time." A few days later we had a phone call, which we related to her. Jaime, a friend of ours, was praying for Lynda. He said he had a (spiritual) picture and he doesn't get them very often! He saw a beautiful beach with white sand and a crystal clear sea. The beach seemed to stretch on forever. At the back of the picture was the Lord, who was radiant. He was walking along the beach away from Jaime, and with him was Lynda. They were going towards a white house. He could feel the peace and knew the Lord was taking Lynda to a better place. The Lord had seen her longing for the beach and answered.

A Sister, visiting one afternoon, found Lynda quite animated. With a huge effort of self-control she listened calmly, as Lynda excitedly told her that she had found the music for going in and out of the crematorium. Would she listen to it with her? She had chosen music by Rutter – very beautiful, very much "her" – going in, "Loving Shepherd of Thy Sheep", and, "something joyful for going out, 'I will sing with the Spirit'." This opened up the subject of her funeral and she talked about us finding a beautiful place in our garden for her ashes. The Sister suggested a simple wooden cross to mark the spot, with her name on it. Her face lit up. Her body would be in our chapel, close to us, before a service at St Mary's Church. Ann, the specialist nurse, had joined us by now. We all three agreed that we hated the crematorium and we assured her that we wouldn't be there long. She had thought through herself that there would be difficulties with a coffin in our garden (space and special permission), so she had opted for cremation. The Sister who visited in the evening had been forewarned so it was slightly easier for her. Lynda said to her, "Were you told?"

Next it was the service – she wanted the Sisters to sing three times. Her first choice was the Holy Island Song:

If life will ebb or if it will flow.
The Risen Christ will with us go.[5]

Next, a setting of some words of St Augustine on heaven:

All shall be Amen and Alleluia.
We shall rest and we shall see,
We shall see and we shall know,
We shall know and we shall love,
We shall love and we shall praise:
Behold our end, which is no end;
Behold our end, which is no end.[6]

As one writer says, "Such is the heaven for which we are created."[7] Lynda had written a little note beside this second song – "Because it shall be." Both of these songs were her very beautiful compositions.

She chose the third song because she saw death as "The Dawn", which was the title. This was written and composed by one of her Sisters.

The dawn of the day shall break,
The sun from heaven shall rise upon us
   Giving light to those in darkness,
   Giving light to those in darkness,
Guiding our steps into the path of peace.[8]

We felt this was a big ask, as we knew we would all be very upset. She was quietly confident we could do it and, when it came to it, we did. She left the rest to us but seriously warned us that we must choose hymns that everyone could sing! It was as if, that dealt with, she put it out of her mind. We kept our tears until we left her room. One kind word from a nurse on the way out was enough to start the flow and then some of the nurses started to cry. A nurse said that she had to come out of her room quickly that morning. Some of them had known and loved Lynda for years. It was decided, "No kind words," as being the safest.

She was very brave but alongside this, the night nurses were becoming increasingly concerned about her anxious, wakeful nights. We talked with Lynda about it. It had begun when she realised that she was having difficulty taking a deep breath. Her fear was not of death, but the bit in between, and especially the breathing. We shared this with the doctor. He held her hand, reassuring her that they would take care of her, that she would become more and more sleepy. They started her on a small amount of oxygen through the nose. Lynda seemed content with that. We also started to go in around the clock, even through the night, taking it in turns to sit with her.

She had been asked whether she wanted to stay conscious to the end, or drift into unconsciousness. She chose the former, saying to us privately, "I hope that I have made the right decision." Attached to various tubes and equipment she was able to move very little but she thought of Jesus in fetters and bands. She felt like him, but knew that soon there would be a mighty breaking free into resurrection life. We talked much about the resurrection body and how her body, which was slowly breaking down, would soon be discarded. She wanted us to know that she didn't regret the choice she had made (to be a Sister of Jesus Way). It had been a good life.

There were other little gifts of love along the way. She had to go down for an X-ray and Fiona, the radiographer we knew, held her hand. On Holy Saturday we all gathered in Lynda's room for a healing service. Bishop Peter anointed Lynda with oil. Laying hands on her, we prayed. Three of the Sisters were in tears and the remainder struggling. We sang a very shaky blessing at the close.

Our 92-year-old Sister Divina, helped by another Sister, managed to speak to Lynda on the phone – all the way from Germany. Lynda could hardly believe it. She was overjoyed and near to tears. Sister Divina said to her: a light was approaching, and it was Jesus. She would fall asleep and wake up in the presence of her Heavenly Bridegroom. She continued that twice she had had the verse, "It is me, do not be afraid."[9] She was sure that she had been given these verses for Lynda. Lynda was, "now in the storm, but not to be afraid". Miraculously, she in turn was able to hear Lynda, as Lynda's voice by now was very weak.

Two Sisters travelled to Wrexham for her parents, as her father was unable to drive because of an operation. It was very difficult for them. At a subsequent visit we talked together in the downstairs cafeteria. Lynda's mother could see that Lynda had accepted, and, in accepting God's will, found peace. She then asked, "And you have accepted it." This was more of a statement than a question. The Sister replied, "Yes." They were overcome by grief. Lynda was their only daughter. Her brother, who lived in Chester, also visited.

We had already begun a pattern of praying our night prayer with Lynda each evening. Often we turned to the Bible. We have a note, "Tonight, talked about, 'Today, you will be with me in Paradise'."[10] Then she added, her old organised self, "On a practical note, could you cancel my dental appointment in May!" Other times we talked about heaven, angels, Jesus coming to her, the light. We read again about Jesus coming over the stormy waters to the disciples. Often we spoke about the Good Shepherd who loved his sheep.

She asked us to bring in the words of,

Haste, haste my soul to heaven,
With Christ I yearn to be.[11]

We cherished these last conversations together knowing that soon they would be impossible:

"Do you think there is anything in me so that the Lord Jesus won't come for me?"
"He took all our sins on the cross."
"That's right."
"The Lord Jesus loves you very much."
"That's what Sister Divina said – he loves me dearly."

In the midst of all her suffering she was still thinking of others. She was concerned that we were getting enough rest. "I hope for your sakes and for mine that it won't be long." She never failed to thank the nurses for each thing they did. One Sister thought, "She is gaining her crown."

It was now the end of April, a beautiful, balmy spring. In the hospital room we could see Lynda's body beginning to break down. The cancer was causing her abdomen to swell and become distorted. She was becoming sleepier with little bursts of wakefulness. She was still keeping her own hands on her medication, pillows and other matters and, in a gentle manner, was directing the nurses! Her memory was better than ours. She suggested to one of the Sisters that she write these things down because, "I won't be able to do it much longer."

She spoke often of wanting to go to heaven and once she added hastily, lest we think she wanted to leave us, "You do understand, don't you – I don't want to leave you all." Of course we understood. She told us that she had heard music; the words she heard were, "Amen, amen." She sang the heavenly music to five Sisters who were with her.

The Gates of Heaven Open

"'Quickly,' said the Lord Jesus and called His angels: 'Come and open the gates – I expect a special treasure of my heart – a real bride, Lynda.'"[1]

The first days of May were all that Lynda would have loved, blossom burdening the hedgerows and trees bursting into fresh green leaf. Spring flowers from our garden brought hope each day into the room. Lynda loved camellia. She had been given a plant for her bridal consecration. A Sister brought the beautiful, deep pink flower into the hospital and we placed it on the little table at the foot of her bed – a symbol of the promises that she had made, and kept faithfully, to her Heavenly Bridegroom.

Two Sisters were now with Lynda day and night. There were heart-stopping moments when her breathing became so shallow that we thought she was slipping away, and then she recovered. The nurses on Conway Ward were loving and kind, taking care of us, as well as Lynda. We waited, and watched with her for heaven's gates to open. Sisters slipped in and out throughout the day. Now we had stopped our visitors, a number of Sisters were able to share evening prayer with Lynda in the hospital.

Graeme, our vicar, was quietly supportive and Dave, the hospital chaplain, was often with us. He wasn't allowed to be too much the chaplain! Only barely managing to suppress her still incorrigible sense of humour, she gently put him in his place with a mischievous smile. He was her friend, rather than in his official capacity. Bishop Keith and Bishop Peter fitted us in at the close of busy days. We were grateful when they were with us, praying, reading the Bible, or sitting quietly by her bed. The emails kept pouring in. We continued to read each one to her.

Lynda's constant refrain was, "I can't understand why the Lord Jesus isn't coming for me." She wanted it all to come to a closure. Her drugs were changed to control the pain. Her mind stayed alert. At lunchtime she tried some ice cream and jelly. She said to the Sister with her, "What am I going to do, eat or die?" The reply came firmly, "Eat!" A day or two after this she was past eating. She was still hearing beautiful music. One morning it was an organ. The peace of God was with us. Her distraught parents and her brother visited late one evening. A nurse quietly allowed her brother first and then her parents to her bedside. It was an emotional farewell, Lynda managing to come round sufficiently to say her good-bye to them, conscious of their grief but now unable to reach out. We stopped sleeping in the room provided by the hospital but dozed on chairs beside her. It was becoming increasingly difficult to hear what she was saying but, knowing her well, we could usually make an accurate guess. We were sometimes rewarded with a lovely smile of recognition.

A porter who had known Lynda for many years came for a last glimpse of his singing angel. He left the room visibly moved. One of the cleaners said that she had prayed for Lynda all night. Then another bravely came into the room to clean it and tell us, she was praying for Lynda. Like Jesus, the ordinary people loved her. We sat quietly, or listened to music from "Jesus, O Joy Eternal"[2] on the player. She never wearied of listening to the gentle music and the soothing voice of Mother Basilea. Lynda was weaker, but trying to help us moisten her mouth with a refreshing wet sponge on a stick. We read to her some of her favourite verses from Scripture: 1 Peter 1, the first letter of John. "How great is the love that the Father has lavished on us that we should be called children of God."[3] "God is love."[4]

The WRVS trolley came around. One of the Sisters discovered that, on autopilot, she had laid down her purse, who knows where? A search began. Lynda looked almost unconscious but with a supreme effort she tried to speak and it was to the Sister, "Be careful!" It wasn't meant only for that incident. It was for the future and in the unspoken communication she knew what Lynda was saying. Be careful, for the sake of the other Sisters. They need you. The promise to be careful was given. A film of tears covered her eyes. Her head sank back after the effort of speaking; her breathing became so shallow that we thought she was leaving us.

Bishop Keith arrived. We were pleased to see him. He sat quietly with us, read from the Psalms and prayed. In the evening the Sisters came and we read our Night Prayer together. Afterwards we sang:

When the midnight meets the morning,
Let me love you even more.

May this journey bring a blessing.
May I rise on wings of faith,
And at the end of my heart's testing
With your likeness let me wake.[5]

Some of the Sisters sang the blessing that Lynda had composed, "My peace I leave you, my peace I give you."[6]

Sunday dawned. Sunshine poured in the window in the early morning. The familiar hospital routine took over. Lynda's breathing was regular but shallow. We could see the ominous spread of the fluid in her body. The Sisters came in. We often sang to her, as she had sung to many patients in this hospital. About 8.45 p.m. Angie, our dear nurse-friend, arrived and stayed for almost an hour. It was lovely to see her. She was her usual self – full of humour, compassion and life. She is totally irreverent, but full of faith! She told us about the times she had nearly died and each time she had seen a beautiful bright light and crowds of people she knew. She couldn't wait to get there but she was rejected (twice). She said to Lynda, "Twice now you've been rejected." She was referring to the time that Lynda had nearly died in our garden and also when the chemo caused the anaphylactic shock.

"When the angels come next time, you go with them, third time lucky!" It was impossible not to smile.

The next day we managed a brief conversation with Lynda – by means of almost imperceptible nods and a few clear words. We spoke about heaven, what Angie had said and more. Lynda went to sleep. The Sisters came in later and quietly sang,

May the angels lead you into Paradise,
may the martyrs receive you at your coming,
and lead you into the holy city, Jerusalem.[7]

Her breathing was irregular. Then it settled down again. Our evening callers continued. Bishop Peter arrived shortly before 9.00 p.m. Lynda held two of his fingers and fell asleep as he talked.

Ann came in the next morning. She noticed that a film had formed over Lynda's eyes and she ordered eye drops for her. We now had two specialist nurses, as Agnes had taken Ann's place one weekend and now she couldn't bear to let go of this special patient. Sometimes they came together. We loved them both. Lynda was unable to move, as her body was weighted down with fluid. Ann was back in the afternoon. She sat and chatted. Dave arrived and left. Lynda came round and began to speak. We clearly heard the phrase – "so slow". We asked if she was saying that Jesus' coming to her was so slow, and she said, "Yes." We were relieved to see Bishop Keith again just as we were feeling in need of support.

We came to Wednesday. In the afternoon Lynda worsened. Ann sat with us, in tears. Lynda said only one thing, and it sounded like, "Hark, the herald." The word herald especially was quite clear. Was it heaven beginning to open – the herald calling her name? Her parents arrived and sat quietly with us. They kissed her good-bye but her mother broke down, as she tried to say all the things she thought Lynda would want to hear. Lynda's hand tightened around the hand of one of the Sisters. She knew it was her parents but could not respond.

We watched with her, well into the night, while life ebbed and flowed. The next morning it was as if she had reached a plateau. She indicated how stiff she was and tried to exercise her arms. We said our morning prayers and peace settled on the room. Sometimes we looked at her and thought, "If only the Lord would perform a miracle. She is so young." The fluid had now reached her lower lip causing it to twist and swell.

About 8.00 a.m. on Friday, she began to lose ground once more. It was 13th May. She said to us, "I am going now." Her mind was still alert. About 10.30 a.m. she hummed a tune that we didn't recognise. When we asked her about it, an excited smile appeared. She closed her eyes and sang the tune again raising her hands upwards. We don't know, but possibly she had heard the angels who were coming to carry her to heaven. Still she lingered. One of the Sisters gently gave Lynda her blessing to leave for her heavenly home. Her breathing now sometimes stopped altogether. Ann again joined us for a short time. Dave came at lunchtime.

It was a quiet afternoon. We had one unexpected visitor, the chaplain from the hospice, a Methodist minister, who we knew. He said to us, "Thank God for the resurrection." He prayed with Lynda, then laid his hands on her and blessed her. Ann again sat with us. We sang, "Peace, perfect peace is the gift of Christ, our Lord."[8] The beautiful words echoed around the room. About 5.00 p.m. we were making arrangements for the evening with a Sister who was leaving when Lynda said, quite clearly, "Are you all right?" We assured her that we were. They were her last words. They summed up her life and her journey through suffering. Her concern to the last was for others, especially her Sisters. She would have been a good "mother" in our community.

When the Sisters arrived in the evening, we again read the emails to her, short, loving messages. Her breathing suddenly became even more irregular. We asked a nurse to come and she gave Lynda an injection to help her. About 8.15 p.m. Lynda gave a gasp and her breathing faltered for about ten minutes. We watched, quietly praying, as the breath left her body. At 8.25 p.m. the gates of heaven opened and she departed from us. Her Sisters surrounded her. We knew it was happening but, nevertheless, there was a stunned silence until one of us said, "She has gone." A nurse came in and confirmed she had died; another appeared with a tray of tea. Their kindness was overwhelming. Both nurses remembered her as, "a beautiful lady with a beautiful voice". We discovered later that a group of Mary Sisters in Darmstadt had been praying for us at the exact time that Lynda died. Some Sisters went home and there was a little time before the car was able to return for the two remaining. We sat by Lynda, peaceful in death, her suffering over. The door opened and it was Bishop Peter. He did not know Lynda had died. The Lord sent him.

Bishop Peter opened his Prayer Book and read Psalm 121:

The Lord will watch over your coming and your going
Both now and for evermore.[9]

The familiar words comforted us. The ancient, traditional prayers of the church that followed echoed eternity, where past and present are held together as one. Holiness crept into the room. A great, unseen cloud of witnesses surrounded us. The Bishop of Chester laid his hands on Sister Lynda of the Compassionate Face of Jesus and prayed a final benediction.

Later as we gently closed the door to her room we paused and looked back for one last time at the still form on the hospital bed, the face we loved dearly. It was the worst moment of our lives.

A Blessing from Sister Lynda

We discovered a blessing that Lynda had written not long before she became ill. The third paragraph indicates that she had adapted it with her Sisters in mind, but originally she had used it in a group she was leading. It is based on the Old Testament Aaronite Blessing. She now inhabits that Celestial City of which she writes. It is from there, radiant, beautiful and healed, as a Sister saw her in a dream two months after her death, that she now blesses us.

This is a beautiful prayer given by God to Aaron and his sons to bless the Israelites. It must have gladdened the hearts of the people to hear it as they faced their uncertain journey through that vast, inhospitable wilderness. It is a priestly blessing and as a member of the priesthood of all believers I would like to pray it over you as you continue your inner and outer journey to the Celestial City!

The Lord bless you!

The Lord bless you, Yahweh, the Almighty, the everlasting Father, for no one can truly bless as He does and He delights to bless!

The Lord **bless** you! May He grant you the desires of your heart! May He give you an abundant harvest, outwardly, of plums, pears, apples, marrows, runner-beans!! And inwardly, may the fruits of the Spirit abound in your life – love, joy, peace, faithfulness and goodness[1] – for the heart of God is a fountain of goodness!

The Lord bless **you and you and you and each one of you**! He has called each one of you by name. The Lord says, "I have redeemed you: I have summoned you by name; you are mine!"[2]

The Lord bless you and **keep you**; may He protect you and keep you from harm as you journey with Him through the valleys of your troubles, your grieving, and upon the heights of your happiness! May the Lord protect you from the evil one, for He is your Good Shepherd who will keep you safe. He will go on ahead of you so that you need not fear. He hems you in behind and before and He lays His hand upon you.

The Lord **make His face shine upon you**. May the light of His face enfold you! May His radiance spread over you, as it did over Moses all those many centuries ago. May your face begin to shine like His. May you reflect the radiance of God upon a dark and broken world!

The Lord **be gracious to you**; for "the Lord is compassionate and gracious, slow to anger and abounding in love".3 May His grace abound to you, His beloved and undeserving child! May His forgiveness be more real to you today than ever before, for His forgiveness flows from His grace.

The Lord turn His face toward you – may you know and feel God's smile, His pleasure over you, His affection for you, for He takes great delight in you, His child. He rejoices over you with singing and He will quiet you with His love!4

The Lord turn His face toward you and **give you peace**. The Lord grant you His wholeness, His healing, His salvation, His Shalom! Jesus said, "Peace I leave you; my peace I give you . . . do not let your hearts be troubled and do not be afraid."5

And so the Lord has put His name on you and me; He has put His special, distinctive stamp upon us because we belong to Him, we are His very own; we are truly his "treasured possession".6,7

Postscript

"Listen to the inward voice of the Holy Spirit. Seek his guidance in all things. There are no blueprints or certainties about the future. Trust in his guidance and wisdom. 'The counsellor, the Holy Spirit, whom the Father will send in my name, will teach you all things.'[1] Jesus said, 'My sheep listen to my voice; I know them, and they follow me.'"[2]

We briefly glimpsed the glory of the Lord and heaven, as the first day of our lives without Lynda dawned. The Lord was close to us, as we composed an email to our friends. Then it was as if the Lord departed. We were left with our grief. There was a sense of unreality. Had this awful thing really happened? A car would draw up in our drive and we half-expected Lynda, fleet-footed, to come through the door. She was everywhere through her absence. Words read long ago came unbidden to mind: "God has trusted us with a great trust."[3]

It had all happened with bewildering speed. Within the space of a few months it seemed as if we had lived a lifetime of suffering. Each one of us experienced loss in a different way: for the Little Sister and the Companion Sister, it was like losing a dearly loved daughter, and for the other Sister who had been with Lynda longest, there was a sense of now being alone, vulnerable, no one alongside her, as Lynda had been. For Sisters who had joined us later, it was the loss of a friend and little mother. For the community as a whole, we had lost a future leader, a gifted Sister who had not yet realised her full potential.

Different in temperament, we all experienced grief differently. Some could articulate their feelings easily, others could not. Some wept easily, others wept alone and others could not weep at all. Some of us found comfort listening to her voice on cassettes and CD; others could not face hearing her voice. We drew closer together in a situation that could have easily divided us, as we were still deeply shocked and exhausted.

The sympathy cards poured in and so did the emails. Strangely enough, it was often those who said to us, "I don't know what to say," that comforted us the most. We didn't know what to say either. We found a large basket and it was soon full to overflowing. It stayed for many months on our sideboard in Bethany. There was support from faraway places, Elias in the Congo, friends in Oman. Nearer home, a tradesperson took the time to email us, writing, "She was a wonderful person." Others, who had passed the time of day with her in the kitchen, were genuinely heartbroken when she died, and came to the funeral. Another told us that he carried a copy of her funeral service (with her photo on it) in his van.

We were conscious of Lynda's parents' grief. Those who Lynda had helped we knew would be distraught. We made an extra effort to trace any we hadn't managed to contact when she was ill. It was as we feared, some collapsing into floods of tears at the other end of the phone. We tried to put our own grief to one side in an attempt to comfort others. There was Nain. We thought that when she knew of Lynda's death we would lose her too. It was Margaret, the matron in the nursing home, who gently told her. Extreme old age had brought Nain resilience, or maybe this had always been her. Like Lynda she doesn't express her emotions easily.

There were practicalities. We were in a situation that was new to us – other communities, because they came into existence at least a century before us, had a time-honoured ritual when a Sister died. We had no such thing. Lynda herself had brought up the subject about two years before her death, suggesting that we should look at what would happen when one of us died. We never did make the time. Possibly there was a reluctance to face our own mortality. We did, however, make wills. At first we had done them in DIY fashion, obtaining forms from the post office. A sense of caution made us show them to our solicitor. That was the end of them! We tore them up. Under his guidance we did them again.

It wasn't that we had much in our personal bank accounts. Each January we share personal gifts of money. This has to last us the whole year for all our personal needs. By December most of our accounts, apart from those belonging to exceptionally good managers, are almost negligible. We aren't bothered about the money, as there is very little, but we realised that there could be complications closing an account, in the event of a death, unless there was a will. Out of sight, out of mind. We forgot the wills.

We were in other difficulties. Who was Lynda's next-of-kin? In the hospital it had been us, at Lynda's request, but did that apply now she had died? We ran into the misunderstanding that can affect all communities. It was almost as if she had merely worked for us. We are a family and a close one, at that. It was Lynda's will that came to the rescue. We rang our solicitor. He stated that because of the wording in the will we were legally Lynda's next-of-kin. At least twice, in the days after she died, we needed to be able to say that, stressing the word, "legally". We thanked God that we had been prompted to make wills.

We collected Lynda's belongings from the hospital. Agnes and Ann were both there, loving and comforting. They told us what to do and before we knew where we were, we arrived in Birkenhead to register her death. We had hoped that Lynda's father would be with us but it happened so quickly we had no time to contact him. Lynda had often, over the years, accompanied both the Little Sister and Companion Sister to banks, solicitors and so on, learning the ropes for the time she would be in leadership. It felt strange that she wasn't there, with her smile, good memory and ability, registering this death. We were still grappling with a sense of unreality. We were asked rather more questions than is usual, such as, were we present at her death? It was the problem again of being a Sister in a community. Eventually we had the document in our hands.

We returned briefly to Clatterbridge Centre for Oncology[4] with a beautiful red rose for each of the nurses. We thought Lynda would have been pleased, as roses had a special place in her heart. We took her best blue dress to the Funeral

Directors. They were so kind that, many times, the reservoir of tears threatened to overflow again. Stuart, our main contact, would ask anxiously, "Are you all right?" We started on all the paperwork. She was one of the signatories on our cheques, her name was the user name on some online services and similarly her name was on insurance documents. We had confidently expected Lynda to be around when the older Sister, who was the treasurer, wasn't. Then there were personal items such as her driving licence and passport. We did the rounds in West Kirby. "Not the slim, attractive Sister who used to come in here?" they said disbelievingly at the bank. "Not Lynda Jones?" the shocked assistants said, as we took her unused medicines back to the chemist.

We were taken by surprise when we were reminded that a collection was made at the end of a funeral service. It seemed utterly alien to us, as we had never asked for money for ourselves or any other cause. We didn't have time to think it through except to instinctively draw back from it. We didn't handle it well. We should have said, more calmly and rationally, that individuals could give anything, anywhere, in memory of Lynda, and indeed we know this has happened but not by our making a collection.

We met to plan her funeral service. Lynda had done most of it for us and we remembered what she had said, "Choose hymns that everyone can sing!" We tried our best! It came together very quickly. We knew that the service must last no longer than an hour and that was exactly how long it lasted.

Our feelings had died but we saw many loving blessings from the Heavenly Father. We decided to invite those who were at the funeral to come back to Redacre for refreshments. We could only guess at the number but in the event it was about a hundred people. Lynda had formerly organised the food when we had big occasions. None had been as large as this gathering. The Sister who stepped in was willing, but needed help with some fundamental questions, such as quantities. One day we "happened" to be in the same place, at the same time, as Isabel, a member of St Mary's who had organised refreshments for large numbers. She had been hesitant to offer her help, thinking that we had it all in hand.

She was a gift from God. The love and prayer from those in our church wrapped around us like a comforting blanket. They always seemed to be in the right place at the right time. Lynda's mother arranged all the flowers beautifully in the church. It was hard for her, but she did it.

The day of the funeral arrived, missing by only a day one of our birthdays. The Lord strengthened us, throughout the day. As we opened the doors of our chapel to allow the coffin to go through, it was a little like the doors of heaven symbolically opening for her. We arrived at St Mary's, Lynda – although it was not really Lynda, only her discarded body – for the last time. Even funerals can have their amusing moments. Our irrepressible oncology nurse, Angie, whispered to her friend, "Wait for it. It will be just like 'The Sound of Music',", at which we followed the coffin into the church, singing, "Haste, haste my soul to heaven". Bishop Peter led the procession and later spoke on the consecrated life. Graeme led the service. Our friends surrounded us. Brian Galliers' widow, Una, sat behind us. The service was all that Lynda would have wanted it to be. In one song, when some in the congregation introduced a second part, the music rolled around the church. We had also purposefully chosen a Welsh hymn, "O the deep, deep love of Jesus", for Lynda's family. There was no mistaking the Welsh singing. We all took part in the service. Lynda's brother Philip read one of her favourite readings, John 10:1–15.

In ringing tones, Bishop Peter proclaimed the Commendation,

Go forth upon thy journey, Christian soul!
Go from this world! Go, in the name of God
The Omnipotent Father, who created thee!
Go, in the name of Jesus Christ, our Lord,
Son of the living God, who bled for thee!
Go, in the Name of the Holy Spirit, who
Hath been poured out upon thee! Go, in the name
Of Angels and Archangels;
Go, in the name of Patriarchs and Prophets;
And of Apostles and Evangelists,
Of Martyrs and Confessors; in the name

Of Holy Monks and Hermits; in the name
Of Holy Virgins; and all the Saints of God,
Go on thy course
And may thy place today be found in peace
In the Holy Mount of Sion:
Through the Same, through Christ, our Lord.[5]

Graeme sensitively led through the short service at the crematorium. The sun shone and afterwards at Redacre, friends spilled out into our garden. Of all our guests, we were pleased to welcome two nurses from Conway Ward to our home.

We chose a beautiful spot in the garden for Lynda's ashes, as she had requested and we had promised. The flowers were a riot of colour. Our builders arrived with fencing they had bought, and erected a fence that enclosed the ground. "A gift for Lynda," they said. A landscape gardener gave us a chunk of sandstone as a base for a small wooden cross. Another friend made the cross. A plaque was attached to it on which was written, "Sister Lynda of the Compassionate Face of Jesus, 1963–2011." Beneath these words we requested the verse, "He gathers the lambs in his arms and carries them close to his heart."[6] Sister Thekla had brought us a plaque from the Mary Sisters. In large letters it proclaims, "I am the Resurrection and the Life; he who believes in Me, though he die, yet shall he live."[7] Underneath are the words: "With God suffering is never the final outcome."[8] Karl and Steve, our builders, attached it firmly to a wall that now formed a boundary wall for "God's little garden". A fortnight later Bishop Keith, Lynda's parents with her brother and ourselves, in a short service, laid her ashes to rest. A Sister, feeling in her pocket, pulled out a card that she had forgotten was there. On it was written, "In this place I will give peace."[9]

"God's will has no why."[10] These words were first voiced to Maria von Trapp in the convent where she was a novice. We, too, had had wise spiritual direction and in the storm we encountered, it held us steady. We bowed our heads, with breaking hearts, to the will of God. We gave him our "yes" – "Yes Father, yes Father, yes."[11] It was not that we believed

God had deliberately sent this awful tragedy. On the contrary, it felt more like an onslaught from the powers of darkness. He had allowed it and he loved us. It was his permissive will. Our yielding was the call coming again to trust him and love him always, whatever . . . We believed through all our grief that even from this, he would bring a blessing.

Many experts have written textbooks on the stages of grief, the same basically as for those who are experiencing a terminal illness. We have always been wary of these books and even more so, when we observed them being followed, almost religiously, by some health professionals. Unfortunately, some Christians have accepted them like holy writ, too. One of the stages for the grieving and for the dying is, "anger". We were not angry: Lynda had no anger throughout her illness. There was no yelling at God, or crying out to a meaningless universe. Throughout we were held in the arms of a loving Father. We follow the Lamb of God who meekly bowed his head and died on the cross. To be angry with God, to us, would have been bordering on blasphemy. We were protected from the meaningless, "Why?" We were sheltered from anger. We are grateful. We were aware, however, that some of our friends were battling with anger at the loss of a young and gifted life. We respected that. This was their expression of grief and love for Lynda. We are all different.

Harder for us, in the cold light of all that had happened, was understanding, if ever we could, the Scripture verses that we felt we had been given and were given to Lynda in the early days of her illness. They all, apart from the verses from the Song of Songs, indicated healing. It is easy to twist them round and say that the healing came in heaven. Of course that is true, but that is not what the words originally meant. We were a community that had built a house on the strength of verses we were given and attempted what humanly speaking looked impossible on many occasions when it was confirmed by a word of Scripture. We knew the dangers of doing this but felt that if this method of guidance was good enough for John Wesley, it was good enough for us! The Lord had always honoured it. Suddenly, it was as if the ground from underneath our feet had shifted. It was a Methodist minister who suggested that when these promises were given they had shielded both Lynda and us. We knew the seriousness of her illness but we – and that had included Lynda – were desperately wanting healing. The Lord did not take away that hope until we were ready. The Heavenly Father had led us gently step by step. This possible explanation helped.

There had been another strange occurrence before heartbreak hit us. One evening at church, our previous vicar said to the congregation, "Has anyone a word from the Lord for the church?" He allowed a time of quiet prayer for listening to God. To her dismay, one of the Sisters, not prone to visions, saw a large sword pointed towards the sanctuary, in other words, the leadership. Her knowledge of Scripture told her that this meant the redemptive judgement of God. She didn't share it. Nothing happened. The next vicar arrived. Within a short time the leadership of the church encountered tragedy after tragedy. It was almost unbelievable that so much devastation could happen to so few people. Something in her knew that we would be next. It was the kind of knowing that verges on certainty. Then, it happened: we were the next tragedy. One cannot explain these things, except to say that there is an invisible realm. If we could only see clearly, it is more real than the world around us. Darkness is not stronger than light. Within every tragedy God allows to touch his children, there is his redemptive purpose. He humbles us, preparing us for heaven and making us more fruitful on earth.

Outwardly life returned to normal. We wondered if it would ever feel normal again. Sister Lynda's name came down from her bedroom door and it felt as if she was dying all over again. Her few possessions were shared between us or given to her mum and dad. We endeavoured to comfort Lynda's friends who came to us, knowing we would never be able to take her place. The beautiful funeral service, which St Mary's had kindly recorded for us, was played again and again for those who had been unable to be there. Copies went all over the country.

Sister Divina covered her own grief to help us with ours. Almost 93 years of age and with a mind that was sometimes forgetful, she still managed to say all the right, strengthening words to us. "The Heavenly Father called Lynda; he had other work for her to do." We smiled when, in the course of one chat, it rather sounded as if there was trouble in heaven and the Heavenly Father needed Lynda to sort it out! With deafness, old age, speaking what was to her a foreign language, English, it is a minor miracle that these conversations took place. For us, it was a comfort to hear her voice even if we had not understood every word! She urged again and again, "You must let her go." We knew this but it was hard to do. A few months after Lynda's death, Sister Pista, who had accompanied us throughout despite the miles between, again sent us a loving note. "How I feel for you," she wrote. We knew that she did because she too had experienced a similar grief when a younger Sister destined for leadership in their Sisterhood died from cancer.

Nain's 101st birthday arrived within weeks of the funeral. The staff at her nursing home sensitively made it a quiet affair. For Lynda's parents and for us, it was almost like a physical pain, as we remembered the previous year, when Lynda had been radiant alongside her beloved grandmother.

On Holy Island, some of us found succour in the rhythm of prayer in the ancient church of St Mary's, as Lynda would have done. The love of many friends surrounded us but grief is a lonely path. We drew closer together, as we honestly shared our sorrow when we met together. Grief still overwhelms us, sometimes when we are least expecting it. A Sister on holiday in a North Wales village heard the lilting Welsh voices around her and burst into tears. It is the unexpected that catches us out. In shared heartache we have drawn close to each other and to Lynda's parents.

The CD was still awaiting completion. Tony, who was convinced that it was special, did not give up! Four months after Lynda's death, and almost two years after we had decided to go ahead, a Sister returned to Liverpool. She was able to correct a few minor errors. Tony acted quickly and copies of the CD came to each one of us for comment. It was then sent to Northampton and on to France to go into production. To our great relief, the CDs arrived here 15th December and with the help of friends, 250 were distributed in one week in time for Christmas.

The Sister who had accompanied Lynda as she sang on the wards, returned to the hospital alone after two months. She had met a nurse from Oncology and found herself promising to return soon. Only the prayer of friends carried her through the door of the ward where Lynda had died. Once she had gelled her hands and walked a few paces there was a loving welcome and her fears eased. She felt that a certain, right sort of professionalism would take over with the patients, and it did. This protected her, yet still enabled her to care for each person she met. Unexpectedly, about 15 months later, after comforting a young woman, she fell apart once she left the ward.

Another Sister came alongside and also took up the chaplaincy work. Now two Sisters again go into the hospital each week. On Christmas Eve, a group of us sang carols on the wards. By sheer chance, our first Christmas Eve without Lynda, we were invited into the room where she had died. It was the only side room we went into that evening. The patient was a dear old lady who was very ill. Her family, broken-hearted, were beside her. We sang for them, as we had sung for Lynda, and the Lord was there.

When Nain was 101, the staff said to us, "Next year it will be a big do!" We looked rather sceptical, as she seemed so frail. However, next year came and we celebrated her 102nd birthday with quite a party! As we write this, she is still with us and now 103! Sometimes we talk with Nain (using writing paper) about Lynda. It gives the opportunity for Nain to express her grief. Quite recently, almost two years after Lynda's death, she unexpectedly asked, "Where is Lynda?" The Sister who was visiting her that day answered, "She is in heaven, waiting for you."

On the first anniversary of Lynda's death, we held a Celebration of Heaven. It was a happy occasion. As Lynda would have wished, it was the Lord Jesus who was at the centre of the day. Someone once said to us, "A community isn't a community until it has a Sister in heaven." We now know what that means. Breaking through into the sadness came moments of joy that Lynda is one of the bright, shining ones, her journey over, perfect in Christ in heaven, healed in every way, free from all that hindered her in life.

Christians in the West do not often speak about heaven. Death is pushed out of sight, under the carpet. Our agnosticism, for that is what it is, serves us ill when we face bereavement. Not many speak easily, naturally and happily about death. The Lord said to his bewildered disciples the night before he died, "If you loved me, you would be glad that I am going to the Father."[12] "If you loved me" – did we love Lynda enough to be glad for her and not selfishly want her back?

It is two years since our Sister Lynda of the Compassionate Face of Jesus went home to God. Already there have been changes in the community. New life has sprung up in many areas. Sometimes we think wistfully, "If only Lynda could have seen this or been part of that." Perhaps she does see. The Apostles' Creed includes the phrase, "the Communion of Saints". We believe she prays for us in heaven. The Heavenly Father is bringing us through our grief and shock. We would hesitate to say that he has brought us through.

C.S. Lewis writes of, "that which bereaves one of the bereavement itself".[13] "The disappearance of the grief is not followed by happiness. It is followed by emptiness."[14] We will forever miss Lynda's face among us. The Lord still says, "As a mother comforts her child, so will I comfort you."[15] By the grace of the Lord Jesus, we are moving forward in his strength. We smile and laughter is once more in our midst. Most important of all, "God is here, near us, unforeseeable and loving."[16]

Notes

Introduction

1   *Common Worship*, The Archbishops' Council 2000, Church of England (alt.)

Early Years and the Journey Begins

1   Ordination Service for a Wesley Deaconess
2   Reception of New Members, *Book of Offices of the Methodist Church*
3   Matthew 6.33, Revised Standard Version
4   Deuteronomy 8.7–9, Revised Standard Version

A Time of Preparation

1   Mark 10.29–30

The Call

1   Song of Solomon 7.10
2   Isaiah 58.11
3   Jean Vanier, *Community and Growth* (Revised Edition), Darton, Longman & Todd Ltd, p. 57 (1989)
4   Jean Vanier, *Community and Growth* (Revised Edition), Darton, Longman & Todd Ltd, p. 55 (1989)
5   "Rule of Life", Sisters of Jesus Way

Early Years in Community

1   Luke 6.26
2   Deuteronomy 8.7, Revised Standard Version
3   "Rule of Life", Sisters of Jesus Way

The Inner Journey

1   Psalm 51.17
2   Matthew 16.24–25
3   Genesis 50.20
4   "Rule of Life", Sisters of Jesus Way
5   Amy Carmichael

Bridal Consecration

1   Matthew 26.7
2   Jeremiah 29.11, King James Version
3   Evangelical Sisterhood of Mary
4   Hebrew 13.5–6, Amplified Bible
5   1 Peter 2.6, Amplified Bible
6   Paraphrase from "You're the Word of God, the Father", Stuart Townend and Keith Getty

Bethany

1   John 14.18
2   Isaiah 65.21–22, Revised Standard Version
3   "A Time to Build", Sisters of Jesus Way
4   St. Francis de Sales
5   "A Time to Build", Sisters of Jesus Way

I Am Yours, Dear Lord, Wherever

1   Amy Carmichael
2   Brother Lawrence
3   St Teresa of Avila
4   Philippians 4.19, paraphrase
5   The liturgy is based on a Jewish blessing
6   "Rule of Life", Sisters of Jesus Way
7   Luke 4.8

Making Music for the Lord

1   2 Corinthians 4.7
2   Matthew 26.39 and 42
3   Words inspired by the Taizé Easter Liturgy

The Bible Comes Alive

1   Matthew 6.2b
2   "Prayer in the Hour of Jesus' Death in Remembrance of His Sufferings", Mother Basilea Schlink
3   Amos 4.1
4   Unknown
5   Irenaeus
6   St Augustine

7   Julian of Norwich

8   St Francis de Sales

All God's Creatures

1   Psalm 121.5

2   Luke 13.34

3   Psalm 36.7

4   Psalm 57.1

Holy Island Diary

1   Psalm 90.2b

2   David Adam, *Flame in my Heart: St Aidan for today*, Triangle (1997)

3   John 15.16

4   John 1.16, Revised Standard Version

5   Ephesians 5.2

6   1 Peter 2.7

7   Watchman Nee, *The Normal Christian Life*, Tyndale House Publishers, p. 56 (1997)

8   John 3.27, paraphrase

9   John 1.51, paraphrase

10   John 4.25–26

11   John 6.19–20

12   Galatians 2.20

13   Exodus 33.14

It is being a Child

1   Matthew 18.3

2   St. Augustine

3   Rev. J. B. Wakeley, *Anecdotes of The Wesleys: Illustrative of their Character and Personal History*, FQ Books (2010)

Visitors, Hammers and Bricks

1   See Colossians 1.4

2   Deuteronomy 10.18–19

3   "St Patrick's Breastplate", ascribed to St Patrick, tr. C. F. Alexander (alt.)

The Dearly Loved Ones

1 All biblical quotations taken from John 21.15–17
2 Music: Sister Lynda, 2007; words closely based on 2 Thessalonians 3.16
3 Numbers 6.24–26, adapted by Sister Lynda from Revised Standard Version
4 Romans 8.37

The Road Winds Uphill

1 Methodist Covenant Service
2 See Psalm 46.1–2
3 Fénelon
4 Fénelon
5 Amy Carmichael
6 Isobel Kuhn, *Green Leaf in Drought*, Harold Shaw Publications (1994)
7 See Hebrews 8.12
8 See Hosea 2.19–20, Revised Standard Version
9 Isaiah 61.3

"God, Me and Cancer"

1 Ecclesiastes 4.12
2 Zephaniah 3.15a, German Bible (paraphrase)
3 Matthew 17.7
4 Peter Volkei
5 Zephaniah 3.15b
6 Richard Daly, *God's Little Book of Calm*, Collins (2007)
7 Isaiah 42.16
8 Corrie ten Boom, *Father ten Boom, God's Man*, Fleming H. Revell, p. 97 (1978)
9 Jeremiah 29.11
10 Richard Daly, *God's Little Book of Peace*, Collins (2007)
11 Judges 6.23
12 Song of Songs 2.11–13
13 Zephaniah 3.17
14 Stuart Townend and Keith Getty
15 Psalm 16.9–10a
16 Isaiah 58.8

17 George Matheson

18 See Luke 22.42

19 See 1 Peter 5.10

20 Richard Daly, *God's Little Book of Peace*, Collins (2007)

21 Psalm 30.5

22 Psalm 30.2–3

23 Isaiah 38.10

24 See John 10.10

25 Psalm 41.2–3

26 Charles de Foucauld

27 Fénelon

28 "Now I Follow", Sister Mary Paul OSB, St Mary's Abbey, West Malling. Sister Mary Paul died from cancer in 2005. Kind permission to print this extract was given by Mother Mary David and the Sisters at St Mary's Abbey.

29 Romans 15.13

30 Deuteronomy 31.8

31 John 11.25

32 Luke 12.6–7

The Singing Angel

1 Horatius Bonar

2 Blessed James Alberione

3 1 Peter 1.3d–6, The Living Bible

4 Richard Baxter

5 David Adam

6 St Augustine of Hippo, *The City of God*, Hendrickson Publishers (2009)

7 Archbishop Michael Ramsey, *Be Still and Know: A study in the life of prayer*, Wipf and Stock Publishers (2012)

8 Words based on Luke 1.78–79

9 Matthew 14.27, German Bible

10 Luke 23.43

11 "Fort, fort mein Herz, zum Himmel", J. L. K. Allendorf, 1693–1773

The Gates of Heaven Open

1 Personal letter from Sister Pista, Evangelical Sisterhood of Mary

2   "Jesus, O Joy Eternal", a CD produced by the Evangelical Sisterhood of Mary
3   1 John 3.1
4   1 John 4.8
5   Margaret Becker and Keith Getty
6   Based on John 14.27
7   "In Paradisum-Subvenite", traditional Latin liturgy of the Western Church Requiem Mass. Setting by Sister Briege O'Hare OSC
8   Kevin Mayhew
9   Psalm 121.8

A Blessing from Sister Lynda

1   Galatians 5.22
2   Isaiah 43.1b
3   See Exodus 34.6
4   See Zephaniah 3.17
5   John 14.27
6   Malachi 3.17
7   Exodus 19.5

Postscript

1   John 14.26
2   John 10.27
3   Frank L. Houghton, *Amy Carmichael of Dohnavur*, Christian Literature Crusade (1988)
4   Now Clatterbridge Cancer Centre
5   From "The Commendation of a Soul", Western Rite
6   Isaiah 40:11
7   John 11:25, Revised Standard Version
8   Mother Basilea, Evangelical Sisterhood of Mary
9   See Haggai 2.9b
10 Maria Augusta Trapp, *The Story of the Trapp Family Singers*, HarperCollins (2002)
11 St Francis de Sales
12 John 14.28b
13 A letter written by C. S. Lewis, in Sheldon Vanauken, *A Severe Mercy*, HarperOne, p. 232 (2009)

14 Sheldon Vanauken, *A Severe Mercy*, HarperOne, p. 231 (2009)
15 Isaiah 66.13
16 Elizabeth Hamilton, *Cardinal Suenens – a Portrait*, The Catholic Book Club (1979). This sentence was one of the reasons he gave for being a man of hope.